Spiritual Renewal

D0325152

Those who embrace the philosophy of holism have long awaited *Spiritual Renewal: A Guide to Better Health in Your Walk with God*. I have discussed the concepts presented with many of my colleagues over the decades. However, I had not, until this moment, experienced the philosophy and concepts presented as clearly as Dr. Lorrie Reed has done in this very insightful work. This book will be a valuable addition to the academic and personal libraries of caring health professionals and paraprofessionals alike.

—Mary Allen Carey, PhD, RN,
Professor Emeritus
College of Nursing, University of Oklahoma
Health Sciences' Center

In *Spiritual Renewal: A Guide to Better Health in your Walk with God*, Lorrie Reed offers a series of pastorally insightful and biblically grounded reflections, aimed at caring for and improving our spiritual "fitness" as women. Her exploration of the holistic relationship of mind, body, human spirit **and** Transcendent Spirit (what she calls the "S-Term") provides a new angle on what is required to be a whole person before God.

Reed includes end-of-chapter devotional exercises designed to promote spiritual equilibrium. Her particular concern for providing "fitness routines" and devotional practices for women who have been traumatized is an especially valuable component of the book.

—Rev. Dr. Christine Vogel
Dean of Students and adjunct faculty
McCormick Theological Seminary
Chicago IL

Lorrie not only calls the restless spirit to accountability, she offers concrete ways of addressing the stagnation that preempts spiritual wholeness.

—Rev. Melody L. Seaton,
Associate Pastor
Covenant United Church of Christ

Lorrie Reed unpacks Jesus' directive in **Mark 6:31**, "Come away to a deserted place all by yourselves and rest a while." This text offers intentional pacing in a world that seems to prefer *doing* over *being*. Those familiar with the spiritual disciplines of prayer, meditation, and reflection are sure to find *Spiritual Renewal* thought-provoking, as a guide for navigating the turbulent waters of ministry. It is a means of maintaining clarity of vision and purpose in chaotic times. A must read for those seeking a holistic praxis for spiritual well-being.

—Rev. Dr. Ozzie E. Smith, Jr.
Senior Pastor
Covenant United Church of Christ
South Holland, IL

Reed has given us a thoughtful, thorough presentation of spiritual fitness and its function as the gyroscope of our lives. Particularly insightful is her understanding of the debilitating power of personal dilemmas such as trauma and abuse and the role of specific spiritual practices in the process of recovery and healing. Her personal poetry, sprinkled throughout the book, is inspiring.

—Chaplain Gerri Mead
Presbyterian Homes
Evanston, IL

Spiritual Renewal is an excellent guide for anyone seeking a better understanding of how to balance their life while enhancing their spiritual walk. This work is also timely because of the economic climate that we are presently facing. Many people are faced with numerous challenges and this guide is a thought-provoking and useful tool in helping people achieve both the natural and spiritual balance that is key to maintaining a healthy life.

—Rev. Joyce Calvin, Founder
Women of Valor Ministry
Chicago, IL

Spiritual Renewal

A Guide

to Better Health

in Your Walk

with God

by Lorrie Reed

HIGHERLIFE
DEVELOPMENT SERVICES, INC

Oviedo, Florida

Spiritual Renewal
by Lorrie Reed PhD

Published by HigherLife Development Services, Inc.
2342 Westminster Terrace
Oviedo, Florida 32765
407-563-4806
www.ahigherlife.com

This book or parts thereof may not be reproduced in any form, stored in a retrieval system, or transmitted in any form by any means—electronic, mechanical, photocopy, recording, or other-wise—without prior written permission of the author or publisher, except as provided by United States of America copyright law.

Copyright © 2009 by Lorrie Reed, PhD
All rights reserved

ISBN: 978-1-935245-05-6

Cover Design: Think Agency

Second Edition
09 10 11 12 13 – 5 4 3 2 1
Printed in the United States of America

Dedication

To my husband who continues to
grow in his faith walk.

To my daughter and granddaughter
who never cease to inspire me.

To my siblings who have come through
the storm with their hope intact.

To my mother who taught me resilience.

To my stepfather who loves God with all his heart.

To the women and children who have
been battered by the storms of life.

To God from whom all blessings flow:

*"He put a new song in my mouth, a song of
praise to our God. Many will see and fear, and
put their trust in the Lord." (Psalm 40:3)*

Table of Contents

Additional Resources

Acknowledgements

THIS WORK WAS DEVELOPED with guidance and support from many people. My special thanks are extended to my husband James, who has been my traveling companion on this fascinating and often frustrating journey of almost four decades. Over time, love has revealed its many faces to us. We have suffered our setbacks and celebrated our joys—often not understanding where our paths would lead us. Nevertheless, by the grace of God, we have pressed on, walking by faith and not by sight. Together we have grown and matured and learned to appreciate and support each other. God continues to mold and shape us as a couple and as individuals. We remember daily that because God loves us, we are able to keep on loving each other no matter what comes.

My daughter Tammy and my granddaughter Celeste have been blessings in my life. They constantly help me to keep it all real and in proper perspective. Often they inspire both laughter and tears—bringing into clear focus our connectedness to each other and our ties to the next generation, and the one after that. They make me rejoice that I am alive to enjoy their presence. They will always have my heart, and I thank God for them.

My siblings remain dear to me and also have inspired me in special ways. Elaine, Wally, and Val have modeled resilience and encouraged me to keep putting one foot in front of the other no matter what. All of us should have been statistics, but thanks to the grace of God, we press on. Though Oscar, Jr., my other brother, didn't make it through the storm, the lessons we learned from him are indelible. He will always have a special place in our hearts.

My sisters and brothers and I have learned amazing lessons about faith and resilience from our mother Juanita. Early in our lives, her commitment to wait on God and her quiet strength encouraged us, and it is doing so even to this day. By the time she made her transition at the age of 73 she had overcome the pain associated with her first tragic marriage and had found peace, love, and happiness with our stepfather Allen.

A variety of editors and other technicians have helped to bring this work to fruition. I extend a special "thank you" to Patti Reynolds and Chris Maxwell. Most of all, however, I give God the glory!

Preface

LIFE IN TODAY'S WORLD can be challenging and stressful. We frequently find ourselves unable to regain our footing. This book is about achieving balance and maintaining equilibrium in our daily lives by cultivating spiritual fitness through regular exercise, involving devotional reading, prayer, and critical reflection. Let's call the process *Spiritual Renewal*. The unifying premise is that regular holistic exercise helps us restore and maintain good overall health by achieving closeness to God through spiritual discipline. Just as in any fitness routine, the process requires that we nourish, exercise, and strive for balance in all aspects of life, including the mind, body, and spirit.

Spiritual Renewal can serve as a paradigm for understanding who God is and who we are in relation to God and the cosmos. As we learn to view the world through spiritual lenses, we become acutely aware of the working of the Holy Spirit all around us. If we are diligent and prayerful, this search will lead to new insight and spiritual transformation. The renewal paradigm can also serve as a problem-solving tool in today's world as we search for answers that are not so clear-cut. In summary, the purpose of *Spiritual Renewal* is to provide a framework for achieving wholeness through devotional reading, prayer, and critical reflection. That framework also facilitates development of habits of mind for getting in touch with God—the ultimate healer and problem solver, the One who can keep us in precise balance and perfect peace.

Pedagogy of the Book

The pedagogy of this book will appeal to readers with a range of life experiences. Those who benefit most from this book will have a desire to cultivate habits of heart, mind, and spirit that incorporate scripture as the primary lens through which they view, interrogate, and evaluate the world. They will be people who wish to engage in habitual study, worship, and praise as acts of devotional discipline. To address their needs, the activities in each chapter will provide such readers with many opportunities to exercise their spiritual muscles.

Benefits to the Reader

As you have probably surmised by now, facilitating spiritual formation is a major objective of *Spiritual Renewal.* Readers who wish to engage in an active process of discernment and spiritual formation will find this book useful in helping them sharpen their skills in areas such as critical thinking, biblical thinking, careful reading, and coherent writing. Devotionals and exercises in *Spiritual Renewal* will help people grapple with their Christian values and with self, during the ongoing quest for purposefulness in life. Additionally, the process of engaging in spiritual devotion will help readers view the world in broader perspective as they draw their attention toward striking a balance between living spiritual lives and resolving the dissonance they experience in physical and intellectual areas of their existence. Through regular and ongoing spiritual discipline, readers will be able to discover who they are in relation to God and who they are called to be. And it will provide them with a regimen for staying spiritually fit.

Author's Perspective

The *Spiritual Renewal* approach draws heavily on my background as a teacher, writer, researcher, and survivor of childhood trauma, who now seeks to help others establish and maintain spiritual well-being. I have been privileged to have some wonderful mentors during my career. One of them reminded me that people feel most comfortable when they talk about what they know. As I was writing this book, it occurred to me that I know about research and statistics and the limitations of the normal curve to account for the whole of reality. I know about learning theory and measurement, about curriculum and teaching, about childhood trauma, and about being African American. I know about people and about the miraculous healing presence of the Holy Spirit. For the most part, I will not be saying anything new. I will simply be reporting on the issues from a uniquely seasoned point of view. For those reasons, I am able to articulate these perspectives with confidence.

My faith tradition further influences my perspective as a writer. Born into the Baptist tradition, I was immersed at the age of seven. As a child, my perspective was steeped in Christian educational traditions of my denomination. Over the years I acquired a firm grounding in faith and amassed a history of service to the church. Yet my search continued. Later, in the process of seeking a better understanding of God, I affiliated with the Pentecostal tradition for several years. There, I received the baptism of the Holy Spirit. More recently, I embraced the United Church of Christ, where I am currently a member. Personally I strive to maintain spiritual discipline, which includes a robust daily devotional regimen with attention to prayer and critical analysis of how I might apply the principles of scripture to daily living. I have tried to make devotional discipline a regular practice involving communing with God as an act of adoration and obedience.

Hence, I have used the *Spiritual Renewal* process as a tool for personal growth, discovery, therapeutic exercise, and problem solving, as well as a way to simply bask in God's presence. It has been through my devotional time that I have been able to lay claim to the healing that Jesus had already accomplished for me long ago—for by his stripes I am healed. I just needed to stop being the victim and learn how to embrace the blessing of wholeness I had received through spiritual discipline. This book represents a way for me to share the process that God has laid on my heart. My desire is to give back to God the very best of what God has given to me.

Speak
© 2007 by Lorrie C. Reed
Inspired by Psalm 40:3

Wake up, Daughter!
It's time to claim your voice in my name.
Speak what I say. Sing what I write on your heart.

Decry atrocities I reveal to you.
Protest violence you witness
As you receive your sight

March to the cadence I hammer on your soul
Do justice; love mercy
Embrace peace in my name.

Hear as I rumble through the earth!
Cower as I bend the boughs of oaks!
Hide as waters cleanse this world!

Hush and hear and hallow
The cries of widows and orphans
And strangers, and others who have lost their way!

Claim your voice in my name, Daughter.
Wake up from your slumber and speak!
Boldly declare the words I write on your heart.

Part I
Overview

Chapter One

Introduction

An Inspired Project

Parker J. Palmer's book *Let Your Life Speak* has always resonated with me. I was in seminary when I read his book for the first time. I found the book to be both disturbing and inspiring. It was as if Palmer had plumbed the depths of my soul and pinpointed my problem succinctly:

> "In families, schools, workplaces, and religious communities, we are trained away from true self toward images of acceptability, under social pressures like racism and sexism, our original shape is deformed beyond recognition, and we ourselves, driven by fear, too often betray true self to gain the approval of others."[1]

Like Palmer, for several decades I stumbled blindly down a pathway in search of validation and fulfillment. More often than not, the only clue I had about which direction to take was signaled by doors that slammed shut behind me as I passed through them. While slamming doors can be disconcerting, Palmer says that closing doors—closing the way—often has a "guiding effect." After reading his book, I realized that my destination—my calling—had been mapped out not by a process of ways opening up before me, but rather by ways that have closed behind me.

One of those ways led me to renewal.

In 2001, I received new life through regeneration of the Holy Spirit. I felt immediately that everything was going to be all right. It was as if I stepped out of a wilderness in which I had been wandering for 40 years. Even as I rejoiced at my sense of freedom, I realized the old paradigms under which I had been operating no longer made sense. That's when I started to scrutinize my behaviors, test my attitudes, and challenge everything that did not give me peace. Over time, I formulated a disciplined process to help me attain spiritual health and equilibrium of mind, body, and spirit. Between 2001 and 2008, this process helped me peel back the layers of confusion; it has given me clarity on my relationship with God. It's as if God put a new song in my mouth. I am eager to share it with all who have ears to hear.

Those who know me well say that I looked and sounded different after my spiritual renewal. My posture was straighter, and I walked with a greater sense of confidence. I was, in fact, at total peace—a peace that engulfed me only after many doors had closed behind me, redirecting my attention so I could see the emerging pathway more clearly. Apparently, Parker Palmer experienced something similar. In order for me to find peace and wholeness, I had to leave my position as a university professor. But that was all right with me, for I had never understood how to be professorial. And I had no desire to learn. Palmer's thoughts about scholarship mirror my own. I was reluctant to be the scholar, and so was he:

> "A scholar is committed to building on knowledge that others have gathered, correcting it, confirming it, [and] enlarging it. But I have always wanted to think my own thoughts about a subject without being overly influenced by what others have thought before me. [...] I am less gifted at building on other people's discoveries than at tinkering in my own garage; less gifted at slipping slowly into a subject than at jumping into the deep end to see if I can swim; less gifted at making outlines than at writing myself into a corner and trying to find a way out; less gifted at tracking a tight chain of logic than at leaping from one metaphor to the next!"[2]

Even as I shunned the scholarship found in formal institutions of higher learning, I realized that being the scholar—processing things through my intellect—was to be my destiny. And my research laboratory was to be determined by God's will, even if that involved jumping into the deep end of the pool.

Ongoing Discernment

After my transformation, I had more confidence jumping into the deep end of the pool. I knew the Holy Spirit was guiding me. Although I have not shared all the gruesome details of my personal and spiritual trek, my journey was marked by gray clouds and high winds, by rejection and abandonment, and by fierce battles and deeply inflicted wounds. Yet, I endured. I survived. And I have thrived because I was spiritually fit. My spiritual fitness was developed over time and with much rigor on my part. As Palmer has observed, this fitness has not come "from a voice 'out there' calling me to become something I am not. It comes from a voice 'in here' calling me to be the person I was born to be, to fulfill the original selfhood given me at birth by God".[3]

After many months of *Spiritual Renewal*, from devotion to devotion, prayer to prayer, and glory to glory, the Holy Spirit has revealed my purpose in small glimpses. Giving me what I needed at the appropriate time. Shedding just enough light for me to see the next step on the journey. The revelation continues, and a gradual transformation has been the result. Howard Thurman expounds on this notion:

> "Despite the fact that I have pinpointed a definite moment of crisis as characteristic of the act of commitment, this is not always the case. The yielding of the center of consent may be a silent, slow development in the life. The transformation may be so gradual that it passes unnoticed until, one day, everything is seen as different. Somewhere along the road a turn has been taken, [it is] a turn so simply a part of the landscape that it did not seem like a change in direction at all. A person will notice that some things that used to be difficult are now easier; some that seemed all right are no longer possible."[4]

Like Thurman, I have been able to look over my shoulder in amazement and see how far I have come by the grace of God. And, because I trust God, I have been content with the uncertainty that lies ahead. I am spiritually fit, and I press onward. These days, I continue to walk by faith and not by sight—understanding that as each door closes, a new one will open wide. I continue to trust the leading of the Holy Spirit, and as I have increased my spiritual endurance I know beyond the shadow of a doubt that everything will be all right. I am guided by my peace.

Implications for Spiritual Formation

The *Westminster Dictionary of Theological Terms* defines spiritual formation as the "evolving growth of one's Christian spiritual life in conformity with Jesus Christ."[5] The Presbyterian Church (PCUSA) provides similar insight:

> "Spiritual formation is the activity of the Holy Spirit which molds our lives into the likeness of Jesus Christ. This likeness is one of deep intimacy with God and genuine compassion for all of creation. The Spirit works not only in the lives of individuals but also in the church, shaping it into the Body of Christ."[6]

This PCUSA definition presumes that people subject to such spirituality have accepted the initial call of Jesus Christ and seek to build a mature relationship with the Holy Spirit through acts of prayer and other spiritual disciplines.

Marilynne Robinson[7] sheds further light on these ideas. In an essay entitled "Psalm Eight," Robinson describes the mystical energy and disturbing emotions that surrounded her as a child. She asserts: "it seems to me I felt God as a presence before I had a name for him."[8] She expounds on times during her childhood when she attended church, sang hymns, prayed prayers, and observed role models enacting the traditions of her faith. Not until she began to ponder and actively reflect on these mysteries later in her life did she understand her spiritual connection with God. Embracing the raw data she had acquired as a youth, then grappling with her experiences and eventually giving order to them, served to put her in touch with the Spirit of God and made her aware of God's eternal grace.[9] The stages of her quest also suggest the rudiments of a process for spiritual formation.

Robinson's insights resonated with me. It is through such rumination that we learn to surrender to the will of God through Jesus Christ by the working of the Holy Spirit. I agree with Robinson that our childhood experiences serve as the groundwork for development as spiritually mature adults. Processing, or "pondering," over our experiences takes place in the context of a discernible logic and order. The remaining chapters of this book will elucidate the process.

End of Chapter Exercises

1. Recall a time when you were at a crossroad in your faith walk. Describe the situation. What were your choices? What did you do? What influenced you to select one course of action over another?

2. Have you ever had a chance to revisit an old pathway after a door had closed behind you? What was different about the second time around?

Chapter Two
Historical Basis for Spiritual Exercise

THE QUEST FOR SPIRITUAL maturity is carried out because humankind possesses an innate desire to reconcile with God. According to one view, reconciliation is facilitated by the leading of the Holy Spirit and involves engaging in works of compassion, justice, discernment, worship, hospitality, spiritual friendships, and contemplative silence.[10] Building blocks for such engagement come from a number of sources. In certain cases, for example, we acquire the essential building materials through catechism in formal religious settings. On other occasions the building blocks are molded from casts of our own blood, sweat, and tears, as prayerfully we endure the vicissitudes of life. Still, in other instances—probably the majority of them—we lay down the foundation for reconciliation by gradually seeking spiritual maturity as we negotiate the rugged terrain of our daily lives. Regardless of the source of the raw materials, the process of attaining spiritual maturity is more than happenstance and cannot be accomplished without the aid of the Holy Spirit. According to St. John of the Cross,[11] if we are to grow spiritually we should "In prayer, come empty, [and] do nothing." The Holy Spirit—not humankind—accomplishes the rest. Be that as it may, given our human need to organize our surroundings, several scholars, mystics, and saints have set out to provide directions for embarking on this journey toward reconciliation through spiritual formation.

Monasticism

One such historical movement focusing on spiritual formation was Monasticism, which describes a lifestyle practiced
by persons who live in seclusion from the world. Those
who practice monasticism seek to abnegate certain values
and behaviors associated with the daily hustle and bustle of
human existence. Egyptian monasticism emerged as part of
a larger process in which men and women sought to develop
their spiritual identity. Before there was a formal movement
known as Monasticism, however, there were simply groups
of monks and nuns who moved off into the desert in order
to find out what humanity was really like when it was in
touch with God. According to Rowan Williams, present-day
Archbishop of Canterbury,[12] they desired to emulate Jesus,
who was in perfect communion with God and, therefore,
believed that human nature could be transformed through
surrender to God in every detail of life. So they assumed an
ascetic-type posture of solitude and quietude, in order to
create a space of stillness and escape from the distractions
of the world.

This may have been the case with the Desert Fathers and
Mothers. In the early fourth century, at the height of Christian
desert monasticism, approximately 10,000 men and women
explored the spirit through daily prayer and reading of scripture in their desert retreats.[13] Their reasons for doing so,
no doubt, varied. Some of them may have fled the towns
and villages as a way to engage in a symbolic, voluntary
martyrdom, which in the early centuries of Christianity was
a principal form of total dedication to faith in Jesus.[14] Others
may have pursued a desire to engage in self-healing, as might
have been the case with St. Basil the Great, following his
brother's death. Regardless of their reasons, these seekers
acted on their faith—a faith that called them to love God in
the highest degree possible. Otto Meinardus tells us that:

"The desert has provided, from time immemorial, a testing ground for the souls of men. Go to the desert for food and drink and you will find a barren waste. Go there to listen to the voice of God and you will receive insight, understanding, and wisdom."[15]

If you think about it, these desert dwellers—the Desert Fathers and Desert Mothers—were just like you and me, needy people struggling to grow spiritually.[16] Their asceticism was used as a tool for disengaging their spirits from the busyness of life, with its dangerous crises and its petty disputes. In quietude and solitude, they reasoned, they were more likely to be able to open their souls to God's divine instruction:

"The first thing one has to do is to keep his mind calm. An eye that never stops roaming about, looking sideways and up and down without stopping, will never see anything very clearly; if it wants to have a good look at any visible object it has to let its glance rest on it for a while. In the same way a man's mind that is distracted by all the concerns of the world cannot find the way to concentrate on the truth."[17]

In a similar vein, Rowan Williams, in his book *Where God Happens*, notes that the great founders of the church were typically practitioners of "the deep inner life of contemplation."[18] Through such a life, they permitted themselves to acknowledge the unknowable magnificence of God as well as the ineffability of God—both of which happen to characterize modern-day mystic traditions of the Christian church. The Desert Fathers and Mothers expressed in simple terms the idea that God cannot be known merely through human thought processes and written or spoken words. God can be known only by love. I believe that allowing oneself to surrender to this love by communing with God in solitude sets up conditions by which emotional and spiritual healing may take place. The wisdom that grew out of the contemplative lifestyles of the Desert Fathers and Mothers was passed down orally at first and later was written down, edited, translated, and disseminated broadly. Spiritual direction, which is described in the next section, represents a modern-day application of the quest for spiritual formation.

Modern-Day Applications

In *Spiritual Director, Spiritual Companion: Guide to Tending the Soul*[19] Tilden Edwards discusses spiritual direction. His book describes ways to nurture the soul as he provides practical suggestions for how to recognize what he calls authentic spiritual companionship. Edwards' major premise is that as people grow in spiritual maturity they begin to see spiritual experiences and events as having the capacity to "show us the nature and guidance of God" not only in our souls but in the all of life.[20] We arrive at spiritual truth, according to Edwards, as the result of moving through levels of knowing when we adopt an attitude and presence of prayer. This knowing occurs on four levels: immediate, heart, descriptive, and interpretive. It involves our whole being, thereby representing a way for us to trust God and be willingly available for God. The Jesuits, no doubt, engaged in the disciplined route to spiritual wisdom.

St. Ignatius of Loyola

St. Ignatius of Loyola (1491-1556) once observed: "Man is created to praise, reverence, and serve God our Lord, and by this means to save his soul."[21] These are the words with which he opens *Spiritual Exercises*. In this work, St. Ignatius attempts to outline for his Jesuit brothers, ways to encounter God and to adhere to a pattern of steps established by Jesus' earthly ministry. The book includes a series of disciplined prayer exercises, thought experiments, and examinations of consciousness, which Ignatius believes will lead to spiritual maturity. The Spiritual Exercises are laid out in a program of practical activities that may be extended over a period of thirty days. Activities may be carried out in a silent retreat away from home or they may be completed "in the midst of daily life, while living at home, over a period of several months." The routines are divided into a series of four movements or stages marked by prayer, visualizations, reflections, and spiritual activities for each week. Typically, participants meet regularly in private with a spiritual director to discuss their experiences and to receive guidance in using the exercises while praying, thinking about what they are doing, and interpreting what is happening to them in the process. Other mystics, such as St. Teresa of Avila, also outlined plans for attaining spiritual maturity.

St. Teresa of Avila

In *Life and Interior Castle* St. Teresa of Avila (1515-1582) outlined a similar—albeit less structured—regimen. At an early age, Teresa's desire for spiritual wisdom motivated her to practice spiritual direction, engage in spiritual discipline, and write about her experiences. Thus, *Interior Castle* records St. Teresa's insights in guiding others toward spiritual perfection through metaphorical use of the soul as "a castle made of a single diamond . . . in which there are many rooms—just as in Heaven there are many mansions."[22] The treatise describes seven rooms or Mansions through which the soul must pass in its quest for maturity and perfection, which lies only in the innermost chamber—"the place of complete transfiguration and communion with God."[23] Initiated by prayer and meditation, the journey mapped out by St. Teresa is not as proscribed as the routes specified by St. Ignatius of Loyola. Rather, she encourages travelers to roam through the various mansions of *Interior Castle* and does not specify a particular length of time one should remain in a single room before moving on. Along the way, the willing traveler acquires certain assets which in turn serve as the building blocks for formulation of other spiritual assets. St. Teresa bases her description on her own experiences, which happen to correspond to accounts of other great mystics, although there are points of divergence. Nevertheless, she makes it plain that she does not regard her description as the only possible route to spiritual perfection; to do so would place limits on God. People of African descent would probably agree that there are multiple routes to reaching spiritual awareness.

African and African American Spirituality

Generally the African and African American experience with spirituality was different from that exhibited in Western traditions of the early church. African religion, for example, was deeply rooted in spirituality. For centuries, the traditional African religions shared a "powerful belief that the individual and the community were continuously involved with the spirit world in the practical affairs of daily life."[24] There was no artificial boundary separating the natural from the supernatural. All the elements of being were united in a comprehensive invisible system with "its own laws, which sustain the visible world and ordinary life for the good of all."[25] And this comprehensive system was transmitted through complex and creative, theological and spiritual mechanisms. For example, these African religions differed from Western traditions, which separate religion into compartments:

> "Western logic has divided the faith into a series of distinctions and categories. Mbiti points out that in Africa 'because traditional religions permeate all departments of life, there is no formal distinction between the sacred and the secular, between the religious and the non-religious, between the spiritual and the material areas of life.' In other words, spirituality is life. Religion is a way of life."[26]

These practices were integrated with Western traditions as African people were brought to America as slaves. For most African American slaves, the Christian religious experience was not only filtered through the perspective of European oppressors but also through the spiritual influences of their African culture. Thus, for slaves who accepted the Christian faith, their experiences became an amalgam of European tradition and the African perception of the world as "sacred and full of the presence of the holy and religion as an essentially collective reality."[27] According to Wilmore, historians "have enough evidence from various sources to establish the fact that black religion in the United States—as in the Caribbean and Latin America—was a resilient form of the Judeo-Christian faith fused to an African base."[28] Even though oppression, exile, and dehumanization characterized the faith, it nevertheless rested on a promise of freedom. For African American slaves, spirituality offered the promise of a better life.

Unlike the European tradition of spiritual formation, the spirituality of slaves was passed down through oral traditions that resounded with promise. Biblical stories, accounts of miracles, and psalms offered hope to enslaved Christian people. Because of prohibitions on teaching slaves to read and write, these biblical accounts were often memorized and passed orally from one generation to the next, but not indiscriminately. Many sources reveal that it was not uncommon for slaves to reject portions of the "book religion" that endorsed slavery, for if a better life was not possible for them in the here and now, it surely would be available to them in the hereafter. For the slaves, "'The Spirit within was considered superior to the Bible as a guide for their religious knowledge."[29] This spirit infused their secret meetings and grabbed hold of their bodies in the song and dance of worship as an act of holistic worship that defied their oppressors and reinforced their faith that the God of justice would deliver them by and by. The quest for freedom is ongoing.

Ongoing Quest to Know Who God Is

As beings made in God's image, we are engaged in an ongoing quest to know who God is, even as we mine for the God-like qualities in ourselves and others. That is one of the reasons we constantly ask the question: Who am I? Howard Thurman reminds us that in answering this question, we may be able to say only this: "I am not sure who I am, but I have given all of me that I can find to the pursuit of this consuming purpose, and the answer to the question is beginning to make itself known, even to me."[30] God has made us intentional creatures, giving us not only body and spirit but also intellect. Therefore, we are committed to addressing this concern for a spiritual identity with all of our faculties. Thurman observes that finding one's identity becomes a single-minded pursuit "that pulls to one point of focus all the fragments" of a person's life and makes that person whole.[31] Thurman further states:

> "Thus a man is driven back upon one of the most ancient insights of religion: that there is a Purpose that invades all his purposes and a Wisdom that invades all his wisdom. To seek to relate oneself to such a purpose and such…wisdom is to seek to know God and to walk in His Way… Thus the Master teaches us that if we seek the Kingdom and His righteousness, all else will be ours. We will not be guaranteed against failure, but we will learn that we may fail again and again and yet be assured always that we are not mistaken in what we affirm with all our hearts and minds."[32]

Recently my pastor preached a sermon about the Kingdom of God and used the analogy of seeds. Pastor proposed that the Kingdom of God is not necessarily a tangible place, but a condition. It is like a seed planted in us that grows and flourishes as our faith increases. I agree with his observation, and I cite the book of Luke as evidence. Jesus tells us that the Kingdom of God is within us:

> "Once, having been asked by the Pharisees when the Kingdom of God would come, Jesus replied, 'the Kingdom of God does not come with your careful observation, nor will people say, 'Here it is,' or 'There it is,' because the Kingdom of God is within you." (Luke 17:20-21, NIV).

The work of the kingdom begins as internal work that manifests in transformation of our attitudes and actions. Like a flourishing seed, this work also becomes evident by the fruit we bear.[33] There are many manifestations of good fruit in the lives of people who believe and trust God.[34] These fruit are like lights that shine in the darkness.[35] The stronger we grow spiritually, the brighter these lights glow as beacons of hope—emanating from the inside out for the whole world to see. The effect becomes contagious as people around us take notice of the change that has occurred within us.[36] These are not attributes or effects that we create and build up on our own. As we embrace the indwelling Spirit of God, we are blessed with fruit that we nurture and develop by the Grace of God.

Spiritual fitness helps us grow in wisdom, love, and knowledge of how to nurture these blessings. Moreover, the indwelling Holy Spirit also helps us resist sin, which is anything that separates us from God. As we are reconciled in our relationships with God, we are transformed by the Holy Spirit, thereby enabling us to become instruments of God's peace, justice, and love in the world. Being spiritually fit improves our ability to attune our spiritual senses and recognize the voice of the Holy Spirit. When we are spiritually fit we live lives of integrity as we embrace the Spirit of God, receive guidance from the Word of God, and undergo transformation through the Truth of God. In turn, it is our responsibility to pass these blessings on to the next generation.

Spiritual strength and endurance are by-products of *Spiritual Renewal*. As the result of developing spiritual fitness we prepare ourselves to use all of our faculties—mind, body, and spirit—to carry out God's will by the agency of the Holy Spirit that was poured out on us when Jesus ascended to return to glory with God. That same Holy Spirit is an inner voice that teaches, comforts, guides, and intercedes for us. As we become more spiritually fit we are able to trust that inner voice to a greater extent. Spiritual fitness then allows us to discern God's will. It conditions us to walk in the light and to exhibit the good Fruit of the Spirit. The Apostle Paul suggests that spiritual fitness entails having the ability to ask God to fill us with the knowledge of his will through all spiritual wisdom and understanding.[37] Spiritual fitness, therefore, enables us to develop the ability to live a Christ-centered life as we try to please God in every way.

End of Chapter Exercises

1. St. John of the Cross has suggested that transformation is the work of the Holy Spirit, not humankind. What are your reactions to this notion? What have you experienced personally, and what have you observed with this phenomenon?

2. Describe some of the ways humans encounter God. When have these encounters been most powerful for you? What has been the outcome of such encounters?

3. St. Teresa of Avila has suggested that spiritual formation is a gradual process with earlier stages of development serving as the building blocks for later stages. React to this idea. What have been your personal experiences with spiritual formation?

4. The Desert Fathers and Mothers believed that God could not be known through mere thought processes or through written or spoken words alone. Describe some of the other ways that people come to know God.

Chapter Three

Conceptual Framework for Spiritual Fitness

Structure of the Spiritual Renewal Process

Spiritual Renewal represents a method of theological reflection structured around the concept of fitness. Steps in the process include nourishment, exercise, release of stressors, and rest. The goal of *Spiritual Renewal* is holistic fitness—specifically, spiritual fitness as part of an integrated, balanced equation for wholeness. Spiritual fitness represents our ability to be perceptive of messages from the Holy Spirit and our capacity to recognize those things that separate us from God. Exercising the spirit stretches and strengthens our spiritual muscles as it prepares us to do God's work. When we are spiritually fit, we have the capacity and tools to resist sin (although our flesh is still sinful) and to recognize those things that prohibit our ability to love God and neighbor. Spiritual fitness exercises prepare us to meet the challenges associated with living in this world. The basic devotional structure of *Spiritual Renewal* includes centering, prayer, devotional reading, silent contemplation, critical reflection, and a method for resolving dissonance by deeply processing the information through some form of creative expression. This chapter will expand on the fitness metaphor and describe in greater detail the steps involved in the spiritual fitness regimen we call reflective renewal, or *Spiritual Renewal*.

Information abounds to define and prescribe mental and physical fitness. Less information exists regarding spiritual fitness. Nevertheless, whether we are talking about mental, physical, or spiritual fitness, a number of common components are necessary to maintain well-being. One of those components is nourishment. Nourishing the mind might involve life-long stimulation of the mental faculties. With regards to the body, nourishment entails providing nutrients through diet or dietary supplements as well as adequate fluids necessary to sustain growth and development of the physical organism. In a similar way, a well-nourished spirit thrives on prayer and receptivity. Nourishing the spirit also entails applying scriptures to daily living, especially since spiritual things are not discerned in our natural thought process.

This concept of fitness requires engaging in exercise on a regular basis. This book is based on the premise that the mind, body, and spirit all need to be exercised with regularity. For example, the mind is stretched by resolving cognitive dissonance, critical thinking, visualizing, and connecting old information to new. The body receives exercise through physical activity that is planned, structured, and repetitive for the purpose of conditioning the body. Physical exercise also improves health and prolongs life. Exercising the spirit, on the other hand, entails reading and meditating on scripture, praying, and critically reflecting on what is read in an effort to apply scriptural wisdom to contemporary life. Trusting in God to work through the Holy Spirit to transform us is also a form of spiritual exercise.

Additionally, the mind, body, and spirit all require respiration to maintain fitness. To respire is to inhale or exhale. The mind respires through processing information as it assimilates or accommodates new ideas. Mental respiration occurs through release of emotional tension. In a physical sense, the body breathes in order to survive as it undergoes metabolism during and after exertion. Spiritual respiration involves inhaling deeply of the spiritual breath of life that quickens us and exhaling spiritual tension and anxiety—that is, casting our cares on the Lord. Renewal and restoration of our energy and strength are the result in all three dimensions. Recovery and restoration also connote balance and equilibrium of vital components of the living system. This might be accomplished through recreation or rest, as the mind, body, and spirit are replenished through sleep, play, amusement, or relaxation. A sense of tranquility and peacefulness is the result of such renewal. Each component—mind, body, and spirit—has its distinct indicators of fitness, yet at the same time all components are linked in complex ways. Because of these linkages, balance among all of the components is critical. Various components of fitness in each dimension are described in the following sections.

Mental Fitness

Mental fitness is defined as a state of emotional and psychological well-being. Indicators of mental health can be seen in individuals who are able to use their cognitive and emotional capabilities effectively, to function in society and meet the ordinary demands of everyday life.[38] The mind is linked to the rest of the body in complex ways. Like any other living organ, the mind requires nourishment. Feeding the mind may entail providing new input on a regular basis. Furthermore, like a computer, the mind's data bases must be nourished frequently with refreshments such as prayer, reflection, music, creative writing, and visual art. To remain vibrant this complicated instrument called the mind also requires exercise on a regular basis. Through reading, life-long learning, and the introduction of new stimuli involving critical and complex thinking the mind is better able to process the deep questions of life with the guidance of the Holy Spirit. Moreover, the mind functions best when it is in sync with the body and the spirit. From a theological standpoint, this has implications for spiritual transformation. Through the renewing of the mind we are in a better position to discern that good, acceptable, and perfect will of God—the One who blessed us with this amazing faculty.

Physical Fitness

Much has been written about physical health and fitness. Keeping the body vibrant and free from disease is the goal. Fitness, then, entails freedom from illness and is accompanied by the ability to function efficiently and effectively, enjoy leisure, and cope with emergencies. Indicators of physical health include body composition, cardiovascular fitness, flexibility, neurological efficiency, muscular endurance, and muscle strength. People who are physically fit possess appropriate levels of agility, balance, coordination, power, reaction time, and speed.[39] An excellent way to maintain physical well-being is to provide the body with exercise, nourishment, and balance. Information about how to do this is readily available. For example, physical well-being involves attending to the body's physiological needs by getting regular health checkups, taking prescribed medicines, eating balanced meals, relaxing, and managing stress. The body is the temple of the Holy Spirit. We should strive to offer our bodies as a living sacrifice—holy and acceptable to God as an act of spiritual worship.

Spiritual Fitness

Spiritual fitness is harder to define. One source has noted "spiritual well-being can be seen in the person who finds meaning and purpose in life, and who operates from an intrinsic value system that guides both life and decisions."[40] According to the Evangelical Lutheran Church of America (ELCA), spiritual fitness is wholeness resulting from being in balance and intentionally nurturing all aspects of health surrounded and supported by spiritual health.[41] The ELCA has specified several indicators of spiritual health that include loving God with heart, soul, mind, and strength. Further they note: "nurturing your relationship with God through daily prayer or devotion is the first step. Knowing that God is always present and has given us the gift of grace through the death of Jesus Christ allows us to stumble along the way and keeps us from getting lost."[42]

The writer of a recent *Upper Room* devotional has also attempted to define spiritual health. She states: "The secret of our spiritual health lies in our times of personal fellowship with the Lord, through prayer and reading God's word...When we omit this time with God from our daily routine, our spiritual life stagnates and weakens, like a neglected plant in exhausted soil." [43]

How are emotions and physical symptoms related to the spirit? Just as the body can indicate emotional distress, our emotions can give us clues to the sources of our spiritual unrest. In spiritual parlance this might be referred to as conviction of sin. Conviction is that disquieting feeling we get when something in our spiritual dimension is not right. Conviction occurs when the Holy Spirit disturbs us with unrest in our innermost being. It is a persistent nudging sensation that begs our attention and urges us to explore, confess, repent, and resolve. Only then can we find peace.

Many people tend to care for the mind and the body but neglect the spirit—that component of our being that relates to the transcendent person. Spiritual fitness demands exercise, nourishment, and balance just like the other two aspects of the human being. Our spirits are strengthened and liberated when we exercise regularly through worship, prayer, reflection, journaling, and other acts of devotion. When we are spiritually fit, we are able to maintain faith in the face of mental and physical challenges. Exercising our spiritual muscles keeps us in tune with the Holy Spirit, and as the weight gets heavy on one side of life's equation we are able to balance the load through faith and trust in God. Not only that, when we exercise we are better prepared to flex our spiritual muscles, as we strive to be more in tune with God's purposes for our lives.

As mentioned earlier, the human spirit is transcendent; that is, He goes beyond the limits of physical and psychological understanding. In that regard, He is extraordinary;

He surpasses the boundaries of the natural world. As a transcendent force, many concepts might be used to help us understand its essence. The human spirit, which yearns to connect with God, was breathed into us by God. Our human spirit engages with the indwelling Holy Spirit, and the Holy Spirit governs the human spirit—not the other way around. For example, the Holy Spirit searches the mind of God, and represents the essence of God. The Holy Spirit is immortal, invisible, invincible, and intangible; yet He possesses a vitality that links every living thing. He is the energy that pervades life, the dynamism that animates life, and the force without which there is no life. He is the third person of the eternal Godhead, the God in us, the all in all—the spirit is ethereal and, at the same time, robust.

Theologian Diana Eck has examined the Holy Spirit in light of Christianity, Buddhism, and Hinduism and concluded that "the stories of the touch of the Spirit are as many as there are individuals and communities."[44] I agree with her conclusion and endorse her observation that to be touched by the Holy Spirit requires our ability to surrender to the presence of God. In addition, Eck associates the Holy Spirit with power and mystery that is universal, active, and relational.[45] She observes that the Spirit is "as intimate and abiding as our breath, as elusive as the wind, as powerful and consuming as fire, and as surprising and mysterious as a sudden sense of presence."[46] Furthermore the Spirit often works in ways that surpass human understanding. Eck advises Western Christians that getting in touch with the Spirit involves taking "a journey inward,"[47] a journey that may entail being quiet, still, and attentive—engaging in a kind of watchfulness and receptivity.

Holistic Fitness—Life's Gyroscope

Fitness of mind, body, and spirit leads to wholeness. We can look at the *Spiritual Renewal* process as one that promotes holistic well-being. Metaphorically, we can describe the notion of spiritual fitness in terms of the gyroscope, a navigation instrument used specifically to bring about stability. The gyroscope consists of a wheel mounted in a ring so that its axis is free to turn in any direction. When the wheel is spun rapidly, it keeps its original plane of rotation, no matter which way the ring is turned. Historically, gyroscopes have been used as a way to keep moving ships, airplanes, and other large vessels level. Spiritual fitness, when cultivated in the context of holistic fitness, can serve as the gyroscope in our lives, bringing about equilibrium, wholeness, and hope through Jesus Christ.

Maintaining Fitness as an Act of Integrity

Maintaining fitness of the spirit also entails sustaining faith in the face of emotional and physical challenges. When we find ourselves off center, we naturally seek to restore our equilibrium in various ways. Affecting balance requires us to engage in renewal from time to time by processing and releasing those things that bind us, and liberating them through acts such as grieving, praise, renewal, and celebration. I contend that observing spiritual fitness and paying attention to transcendence, facilitates the well-being of the entire human organism. When we exercise for spiritual fitness, we are seeking integrity in our lives.

Not too long ago, I read an article in the publication *Alive Now* that described the concept of integrity as it relates to communities of faith. The article provided a definition that seems fitting for a discussion about holistic fitness:

> "A call for integrity is a call for consistence between beliefs and actions, between words and deeds. Integrity gives evidence—evidence that our lives demonstrate the conviction, commitments, and loyalties we claim to embrace. From a faith perspective, integrity shows congruence between the lives we live and the values and expectations we adopt in our spiritual journey—whether we identify with a particular tradition or not."[48]

Integrity, equilibrium, and balance are all words that aptly describe the concept I am attempting to share. Maintaining the integrity of mind, body, and spirit represents a condition in which the components of our ecological environment coexist ideally. In God's infinite wisdom we were blessed with a mind, a body, and a spirit. To focus only on the mind or the body and to disregard the spirit is to ignore the wondrous mystery of God's creation and to squander the potential God has placed within us.[49] Hence we are given the power to express our love of God through living lives of integrity. If we do so, everything else falls into place. Restored into place are the wholeness, balance, and equilibrium that were ours when, in the beginning, God blew breath into us and we became living souls. Regular exercise moves us toward wholeness— advancing us toward unity and oneness with God.

Chapter Four

Holistic Fitness and Synergy

Synergy in Relationships

Theologian Leo Boff reminds us that everything exists in relationships.[50] He says: "From an ecological viewpoint, everything that exists co-exists. Everything that co-exists pre-exists. And everything that co-exists and pre-exists subsists by means of an infinite web of all-inclusive relations. Nothing exists outside relationships."[51] I believe by extension of his argument that those relationships must be held in equilibrium. When we neglect the spirit, for example, we end up placing more weight on the mind and body than they were meant to bear. Howard Thurman states:

> "There is an essential harmony in all existence, and the life of every living thing shares in it. Man co-operates with the Spirit of God by making himself open and available to it. And this fact is crucial. A man may elect not to do this and thereby create for himself many problems of inner chaos and confusion; these may or may not be assessed as such."[52]

A conclusion we can draw from these two theologians is that there exists a delicately balanced relationship of mind, body, and spirit. From time to time, the balance among these dimensions is thrown off by unexpected developments in our world. This could happen for a number of reasons. Sometimes we're not so sure anymore of a thought we once believed. Medical and other scientific breakthroughs might give us a false sense of mortality or immortality. Death, suffering, or natural disaster might shake our sense of certainty. Restoring the equilibrium requires that we scrutinize all of the available information and formulate an equation that will result in our well-being overall—thus allowing us to proceed through life with some sense of balance.

Holism and Equilibrium

Achieving equilibrium in human relationships hinges on the very idea of synergy. From one perspective, the human being consists of a highly structured ecological system. Change in any one subsystem requires adjustment in the other subsystems. When these systems are out of balance, dissonance is the result. Using another example, the mind is responsible for the intellect, emotions, and the will. Dissonance might arise when we experience emotions such as anger, disappointment, shame, guilt, unhappiness, or displeasure. And, quite often, the emotions can trigger disquiet in the body and spirit. Our systems make every effort in these instances to restore the harmony that is missing. To live life holistically is to strive for balance in all things.

In my former work as a quantitative researcher, I examined complex relationships among variables using correlation as a prediction tool. After examining preliminary information, I formulated hypotheses for predicting an outcome to the question or problem I was trying to address. The one thing that struck me in every case was that these hypothesized prediction equations always contained an error term—something that could not be explained by the known variables or by their interactions with each other. This suggested that the whole was always greater than the sum of its parts. The more I studied these relationships and examined them through theological eyes, the more I began to ask: Could the so-called "error term" be the spiritual dimension in life's equation? Examining these notions can help shed light on holism with respect to mind, body, and spirit.

Let's apply the concept of prediction to the notion of holistic fitness. In any given situation holistic fitness is based on the contribution of the mind, the body, and the human spirit plus an unknown factor. Now we know that as humans our attempts to achieve balance will be subject to all types of error. The so-called "error term" in our prediction equation then represents human limitation. This unknown factor accounts for what the mind, body, and human spirit cannot explain or take into account. Therefore, I submit to you that the so-called "error term" in this equation (which we will refer to as the "S-term" for sake of this discussion) is no error at all—it is the working of the Transcendent Spirit in the human life and is a force that can bring about equilibrium regardless of the variables or the circumstances.

Holistic Fitness = Mind + Body + Human Spirit +
Transcendent Spirit ("The S-term")

As we become holistically fit, we become more attuned to explanations that include the mental, the physical, and the spiritual. When the mind, body, and spirit equations of our lives don't account for all the variability we experience, the difference can be explained by the "S-term." What, then, is the "S-term"? It is the eternal term, the supernatural term, the synergistic term, or the Spiritual term. The "S-Term" can take on any value from zero to infinity and in doing so can account for the unexplained relationships among the variables overall. The "S-term" balances the equation and, in doing so, makes the whole greater than the sum of its parts. It gives us access to the fullness of life (abundant and eternal life). And as we become spiritually fit, we become more attuned to explanations that include the mental, the physical, and the transcendent.

End of Chapter Exercises

1. Exercising the spirit stretches and strengthens our spiritual muscles as it prepares us to do God's work. Recall

a time when your level of spiritual fitness was low. How did you know you were spiritually out of shape? What did you do to get yourself back into shape spiritually?

2. We can look at the *Spiritual Renewal* process as one that promotes holistic well-being. What does holistic well-being look like, feel like, taste like, sound like, and smell like?

3. Describe ways in which one's spiritual state of being influences one's physical and emotional states as well.

4. Describe your spiritual exercise activities. What are the strengths and weaknesses of your devotional routines?

5. The "S-term" balances life's equation and makes the whole greater than the sum of its parts. Recall and describe a situation when this principle was operation in your daily life.

6. Recall a time when your sense of balance among mind, body, and spirit was disturbed. What led to the imbalance? What specific things did you do to restore balance?

Chapter Five
Steps in the Process

M Y MOTHER'S GREAT AUNT Belle modeled a kind of *Spiritual Renewal* process for me when I was a little girl. Aunt Belle lived in a third floor walk up on east 67th Street in the Woodlawn neighborhood of Chicago. To get to the bathroom in her apartment, you had to pass by Aunt Belle's bedroom. That's where you could find her every morning spending quiet time with the Lord. As you tiptoed past her door to wash up and brush your teeth you could hear her reading her Bible slowly. She savored each word, tracing the lines of the text with her fingers so she wouldn't lose her place. She would read a while; then she'd hum a while, occasionally whispering the name of Jesus through a toothless smile. Her routine did not change for as long as I knew her. Every day of her life, Aunt Belle took comfort from knowing that Jesus was her Redeemer, her very own personal Savior. She lived her convictions through the discipline of daily devotionals.

How can we learn from Aunt Belle? In the next few pages I will explain the steps in the *Spiritual Renewal* process. Those steps involve centering, prayer, devotional scripture reading, silent contemplation, and critical reflection. Renewal can be enhanced further through use of creative release and additional centering and prayer. Not only that, the whole exercise can be therapeutic, from my experience. Also, you can take your journaling to a new level by incorporating theological reflection, storytelling, letter writing, or poetry.

Centering

Quiet receptiveness constitutes the first step in the discipline of *Spiritual Renewal*. We refer to this receptiveness as centering. Centering prepares us to receive the gift of God's presence through the indwelling Holy Spirit. In our quiet time with God, things tend to fall into place. Background noise ceases—noises like the incessant banter on the television, distractions from conversations that take place all around us, and other dissonance associated with the busyness of our lives. Without all that interference we are able to think better and deeper, gathering our thoughts and letting them flow into a pool of coherence. Centering in silence serves a specific purpose. Howard Thurman describes the purpose of spiritual disciplines:

> "[They] clear away whatever may block our awareness of that which is God in us. The aim is to get rid of whatever may so distract the mind and encumber the life that we function without this awareness, or as if it were not possible. It must be constantly remembered that this hunger may be driven into disguise, may take a wide variety of twisted forms; but it never disappears— it cannot. Prayer is the experience of the individual as he seeks to make the hunger dominant and controlling in his life. It has to move more and more to the central place until it becomes a conscious and deliberate activity of the spirit. When the hunger becomes the core of the individual's consciousness, what was a sporadic act of turning toward God becomes the very climate of the soul."[53]

Centering is a concept that has probably been around throughout the ages. One Psalmist tells us that he was instructed to "be still and know that I am God" (Psalm 46:10). Thus, in stillness and in silence we are able to listen expectantly as we confront our weaknesses and turn them over to God. In such a state of openness we are compelled to let go of those things that weigh us down emotionally and spiritually. We become acutely aware of our limitations. We realize that

we are powerless in many cases to change our own circumstances. We wait. We listen for the prescriptions God sends
us through the solitude and the quietude.

Being alone during this time of centering is important. The
original Desert Fathers and Mothers understood this. The
writings of the Desert Fathers and Mothers make us aware
of the difference between the modern-day pathological loneliness that many of us face as a result of being spiritually
unconnected and what they refer to as "natural loneliness,"
which is creative, life-giving, and full of grace:

> "It is a loneliness to which we all should devote much
> time. We must be able to withdraw ourselves from the
> noisy crowds, which are so superficial, so distracting, and
> so counterproductive—in a withdrawal, which is healthy,
> beautiful and good. It is important that we learn to shut
> off the constant communication with the many, which
> does not allows [sic] us to be alone with our self—and as
> a consequence, we are not able to be with the One who
> is always waiting, the incarnate Logos and God. We must
> make the time and find the way for this other kind of
> sacred communication of natural loneliness. And we must
> pursue this knowledgeably, with an orderly, disciplined
> program."[54]

Rather than escaping to a literal desert, our modern-day
places of quiet and peace are carved out of spaces we identify
as sacred. In our metaphorical deserts, we can seek God, for
the desert is a place where the only thing standing between
us and God is our ability to surrender. Contemplation that
takes place in this manner, according to Rowan Williams,
opens doors for God's healing, reconciling, forgiving, and
creating work to occur. Furthermore, one of the Desert
Fathers reminds us that in any given situation there may not
be a clear answer to our questions, but "the very process of
reflecting and discerning makes space in ourselves for the life
of Christ and the creative movement of God."[55]

It is also during the centering phase that we should pay attention to our breathing. As we breathe we should visualize the day of creation when God blew into Adam the breath of life (Genesis 2:7). Or picture Ezekiel in the Valley of Dry Bones, bones that were quickened by the breath of the Spirit (Ezekiel 37:8–10). We might also want to envision Jesus with his disciples just before the ascension as he breathed on them to receive the Holy Spirit (John 20:21–22). While I engage in this exercise I often remind myself that breathing is critical to life. When a baby is born it does not become animated until it takes its first breath. People can learn to control their heart rates, circulation, blood pressure, and other bodily functions by regulating how they breathe. Also, spiritual life was breathed into us by the Most High. I believe that as one who seeks to know God it is my responsibility to inhale of the Spirit as deeply as I can so that its power permeates every fiber of my being. And it is my responsibility to exhale those things that are not of the Spirit. After only a short time, I begin to sense a feeling of calmness if I am receptive to this grace. Other ways of centering include visualizing, rehearsing the lyrics of hymns in your head, meditating, focusing on a thought for the day, and similar techniques.

Prayer

Prayer is critical to the process of *Spiritual Renewal*, for prayer changes things. Prayer is a form of communication with God. When we talk to each other, we have a better sense of who we are in relation to the other. If this talk does not occur, misunderstanding results and signals get crossed. The same is true of our communication with God. The more we talk to God, the more acute is our understanding of God. The better we understand God, the more we are likely to trust. And if we can trust, we learn to "wait and be still."[56] Thurman observes that to pray is like satisfying a hunger of the heart:

"When the hunger in a man's heart merges with what seems to be the fundamental intent of life, communion with God the creator of Life is not only possible but urgent. The hunger of the heart… can be a clue to the Father's house, to the Holy of Holies, wherein the Creator of Life and the King of the Universe has His dwelling place. Prayer is the means by which this clue is pursued." [57]

Our prayers don't need to be long, creative, or dramatic. They only need to be sincere. Sometimes the simplest prayers say it all. In fact, Matthew 6:5–8 cautions us about the use of empty phrases when we pray. God knows what we need even before we ask. Nevertheless, the Apostle Paul instructed that we should pray in the Spirit on all occasions with all kinds of prayers and requests (Ephesians 6:18). We are told to "be careful for nothing; but in everything by prayer and supplication with thanksgiving let your requests be made known unto God" (Philippians 4:6), and to pray without ceasing (1 Thessalonians 5:17). Scripture also tells us that effectual and fervent prayers are powerful; through them we can be healed (James 5:15–16). Through prayer the heaviness of our hearts can be replaced with hopefulness. We can feel our scarred and broken spirits being mended. God tends to our wounds and gives us the strength to move forward as the result of prayer. The more we ask the more God gives. As God answers our prayers, we learn to say "I trust you, God."

When people pray they don't turn their anger, guilt, or shame in on themselves. From a practical standpoint, prayer allows us to let go of our anger, frustration, bitterness, resentment or whatever negative energy we are harboring. As we release that energy in prayer, God restores us to equilibrium and gives us new reasons to hope. I believe God hears our prayers and answers in God's own way and time. God changes our minds and our hearts. Through prayer, God makes us whole and gives us peace. God will serve as an unwavering force that replenishes our depleted souls over and over again in times of trouble. All we have to do is ask for help.

Focus Scripture (Devotional Reading)

Devotional reading involves spending quiet time reading and reflecting on the Word of God. For me this involves making space for God in the mornings. At first, I devoured the Word in big gulps, as if I were trying to re-hydrate a spirit that had gone without nourishment for way too long. Then I began to consume the Word in smaller portions. That's when I started to savor prayerfully the mysteries and profound truth of what I was reading. Now each reading of the Word is fresh, and strong, and powerful. Sometimes I read for pleasure and inspiration. At other times my reading and reflection are driven by questions as I attempt to apply the Word to everyday issues in my life. Always, however, during devotional reading I listen for the Word of God in Scripture. Gregory the Great (6th century) expressed it as "resting in God."[58] The Bible as scripture holds many lessons for people who seek answers to life's challenges. It edifies, instructs, strengthens, entertains, comforts, and guides. And it helps us to stay spiritually fit.

Silent Contemplation

Silent contemplation is another important part of the renewal process. It involves listening *for* the Word of God with expectancy, and making our self available to hear what God is communicating to us:

> "We remember that God made all things by an act of self-communication, and when we respond to his speaking, we are searching for some way of reflecting, echoing that self-communication. But the same is true in all of our relationships, not just in what happens in worship."[59]

Rowan Williams reminds us, "If we are to respond adequately—truthfully—we must listen, for the word God speaks to and through each element of the creation—hence the importance of listening in expectant silence."[60] Moreover during our quiet contemplative time, we can let our minds focus on selected thoughts, I believe. No one is vying for our attention. We are not under pressure to solve anything or respond to someone else's urgent demands on our time. We are free to ruminate and prayerfully discern more clearly a message from the scripture.

Focus Questions

Each *Spiritual Renewal* session includes questions. Reading with a purpose is an important strategy used in the process. Our inquiries are guided by the questions we ask. Whether these are questions we formulate for our own personal problem solving, or questions provided in the study materials, these probes will draw our attention to aspects of the scripture that help us address the issues we have raised and find the answers we seek. Later, during critical reflection, we will find ourselves recalling the scripture and reflecting critically and spiritually on its applicability to our personal situations.

Critical Reflection

Both liberating and empowering, critical reflection can serve as a catalyst for personal growth, actualization, and spiritual renewal. Reflective journaling is one way to engage in critical reflection. It can serve as a catharsis by helping us bring closure to an episode or an issue. Journaling can also function as a mechanism through which writers explore feelings and beliefs in an attempt to make sense of their lives. Kiesinger reminds us that analysis and interpretation of carefully kept journals, and other documents reveal a curious blend of both the objective and the subjective—woven into a rich, detailed, and self-critical account of one's experiences.[61]

CREST (Creative Release for Equilibrium and Spiritual Transformation)

Another important component of spiritual fitness involves CREST or Creative Release for Equilibrium and Spiritual

Transformation. To crest means to reach the line or surface that defines the summit of something. It might be helpful to look at cresting in terms of rivers that reach their highest point. No sooner than the flood waters of a river have crested, for example, they begin to recede. In the process, the waters will never again have their boundaries defined by the same river banks. After the crest, the river will have a different pattern of flow and thus will be changed incontrovertibly and forever. The same principle applies during *Spiritual Renewal.*

In terms of learning, a crest represents the height of our understanding of a thing *at a particular point in time.* After we have engaged in the process of holistic fitness and have reached a crest, we may still have some unfinished business. But those issues, which weighed us down so heavily before we began the process and which seemed insurmountable upon first glance, will be reduced to something smaller as we examine them in a different light—a light emanating from the Holy Spirit. Both we and the issues will have a new identity and a new direction, in other words.

Cresting also represents an act of creativity. It is during this creative process that we have an opportunity to express heightened awareness of our relationship with God and the Holy Spirit. All of this serves to fortify our sacred identity, according to scholar and theologian Lee Butler. Butler says that redefining sacred identity is based on the premise that "God's grace is at work in our lives restoring our spiritual, emotional, and relational health."[62] Sacred identity formation further entails invoking the ability to respond to "God's gracious transforming presence in our lives;" this ability leaves us open to the grace of God to heal our brokenness and reconcile our relationship with God—based on a wholesome, rather than a scarred image of who God is.[63] In the final analysis, sacred identity formation means striving for continued spiritual growth and being an active partner with God in redeeming the world.[64] In his analysis, Butler suggests that a creative process should be used to examine our historical past, expose any rage associated with these foundational elements of identity formation, transform that rage through creativity, and construct a healthier identity grounded in spirituality.[65] While Butler suggests that this approach can be highly useful for helping African Americans renegotiate their past, I contend that releasing rage through creativity can be a useful tool in any transformational process.

As you will see, poetry served as a CREST mechanism for me. Over a nine-month period, I penned over 100 poems—some good, some not so good. What is important is that poetry served as a form of release for me. I was able to refine my awareness and redefine some of the restrictive beliefs from my past. The more clarity I gained, the more empowered I felt. My sacred identity grew stronger along with my spiritual self-concept. And I was able to trust more in the Holy Spirit, which led me to stop being the victim and to change the self-defeating choices I had been making for myself in the past. In addition to poetry, other forms of creative release include prayer, storytelling, letter writing, theological reflection, dance, music, art, sports, physical exercise, and recreation. Use whatever method of release that works best for you.

End of Chapter Exercises

1. Either lying down or sitting upright, breathe in deeply through the nose, hold it for a couple seconds; and then breathe out through the mouth. Repeat this cycle slowly and rhythmically ten times with eyes closed, if possible.

2. Today we are not able to escape to a literal desert in order to experience the solitude and quietness needed to be in touch with God. What are some of the modern-day places we go to find peace and quiet?

3. It has been said, "prayer changes things." Using lived or observed experiences, describe examples of this.

4. Describe how you have used the steps described in this chapter.

Chapter Six

Activities for Release and Restoration

THIS CHAPTER DESCRIBES SEVERAL forms of creative release—theological reflection, storytelling, poetry, journaling, and letter writing. Although one form of release may be more appealing to you than some of the others, I urge you to try all of these approaches. Each one is liberating in its own way. They will help you develop skills for staying spiritually fit.

Theological Reflection

Theological reflection represents an attempt to convey our feelings, observations, and reactions as we seek to discern God's purpose and to walk in a way that honors God's will. As with most other things in life, there is no one right way to reflect theologically on an issue or concern. In her book *Reflecting with God*, Abigail Johnson[66] recommends a six-step model. Specifically Johnson's model asks the writer to identify selected incidents that have brought about a change in perceptions regarding a particular issue or concern that has been challenging.

Typically, section one of the reflection begins by naming and describing in some detail an event or issue that has generated concern for the writer. Section two adds "another layer" to the analysis by describing how the writer felt, what challenged or stimulated the writer, or disturbed the writer about the issue. Section three digs a little deeper (calling on the writer to expand his or her thinking, so to speak) by reflecting on and exploring core values regarding the event. Here the writer is then asked to make a faith connection. Finally, section four factors in social and/or power issues that may be pertinent to the event by drawing conclusions and discussing revealed insights. Johnson's entire theological reflection process ends with a prayer.

Storytelling

In her book *Beyond Impunity* Genevieve Jacques writes: "Every healing process begins with a time for speaking and listening, so that the victims can break out of the isolation and shame imposed by those who have wounded them, so that they can escape from their obsessive fear, so that they can recover their capacity to live in relationship with others— with people who are able to hear them."[67]

Charles Whitfield advances this line of reasoning:

> "If we commit to work through our pain and grieving, we then begin to share, ventilate, participate and to experience our grief. We may need to tell our story in such a fashion, several times periodically over a period of several hours, days, weeks, or even months—in order to finally complete our story. We may also have to consider it in other ways, mull it over, dream about it, and even tell it again."[68]

Storytelling is a time-honored tradition in many cultures. Stories convey important information to us and to others in ways that few other forms of communication can accomplish. During storytelling, a shift in consciousness takes place, for our remembrances take on narrative structure that might otherwise seem random and meaningless. With each re-telling we are able to add new details to the old memories and deepen the context of what occurred and why. As we reconstruct and reconcile the information, we are forced to get the story straight as we fill in the gaps of a situation. In that regard, storytelling helps the mind to make sense of the world. Stories help both tellers and listeners to reconsider lived experiences in light of new possibilities. In addition, they represent mechanisms for transmitting knowledge, wisdom, and hope from one generation to the next.

In this regard, stories can be both healing and transformational. When we engage in storytelling as a form of *Spiritual Renewal* our version of the Truth emanates from the Spirit of Truth who knows the mind of God. From my own point of view, telling stories also helps us to relive, reflect upon, and reevaluate our experiences in such a way that we can define more clearly where we have been and where we must go in order to be closer to God. Often when we begin to tell our stories, we are prone to "see through a glass, darkly." As we gain spiritual fitness, however, our vision reaches a higher level of definition and resolution.

Poetry as Renewal

Why poetry, you might ask. While prose is fine for business reports and news stories, the everyday language we use is subjective, ambiguous, and embedded in highly personal contexts. When dealing with abstract concepts, lofty ideals, or charged emotions, prose may be viewed as a factor that complicates mutual understanding. In the context of discourse about personal matters, some of the images and experiences we wish to communicate may be too painful, too shameful, or too personal to convey with mere prose. Experiences that gave rise to these images live in vivid color and granulated texture in the places where our memories are stored. More often than not, simple prose is powerless to relate the spiritual essence of the messages we wish to express. Consequently, because prose is subjective, ambiguous, and embedded in uniquely personalized contexts, it is viewed as a factor that complicates mutual understanding.

Poetic communication, on the other hand, is the language that breaks things down to their essential meanings—stripped of their judgments and cultural baggage. If the message of the poem is true, its essence will serve as the skeletal structure on which the readers will add flesh, and dress, and color, and texture from their own frames of reference. Sometimes we are overtaken by thoughts so profound, emotions so pure, and pain so deep that we don't have the words to express how we feel. In this society that values rational, objective expression we are not able to write an essay about our concerns nor are we certain that we understand the facets clearly enough to organize them into a coherent piece of prose. But deep down inside we know how we feel, we know where we hurt, we understand the incongruence of the situation. Expressing all this succinctly through prose is sometimes impossible. Poetry gives us space to express that which would otherwise be ineffable.

Letter Writing for Renewal

Letter writing was common among some of the founders of the early church, such as Gregory of Nazianzus, Basil of Caesarea, and John Chrysostom. I have read some of the letters, which revealed so much about them as thinkers and as people—their deepest feelings, hopes, and dreams as well as their motives for doing certain things. All of this information was laid bare in the pages of their correspondence. They articulated many important theological insights in the bodies of their epistles. Those who set pen to paper, of course, can only hope that the impressions their letters leave will be lasting ones.[69]

This can be seen in the epistles written by Paul to his protégé, Timothy. The insights and information contained in these letters have influenced entire communities of people who have struggled with questions, regarding how to live in harmony with each other as one body in Christ. These letters have endured for hundreds of years; they still direct our decisions. In addition to providing insights and information, letters can evoke strong emotions. They can entertain, infuriate, or inspire. Those letters that have the greatest emotional impact are those which have been written with sincerity and which emanate from the deep, often spiritual, places in the soul and psyche of the writer.

Journaling

Journaling can serve as a mechanism through which people can interrogate their feelings and beliefs in an attempt to make sense of their lives. Journaling entails soul-wrenching reflection, helping the writer not only ask but answer questions. Both liberating and empowering, journaling can work as a catalyst for personal growth and actualization. It represents a means for restoring memory, and the whole exercise can be therapeutic.[70] Jennifer Hollowell describes her experiences with journaling.[71] She notes that each journal entry allows her to process what's important. Her entries allow her to set her thoughts and feelings to paper and to examine them later. She uses her paper journals to explore her innermost thoughts in a place where she can freely express herself. According to Hollowell, "Some days I'll ramble on for pages and pages, while others are just a single sentence." She further notes, "the act of purging through the writing process (be it with a pen or a keyboard), offers a type of cleansing that discussion doesn't seem to solve." Her method of "getting it all out" allows her to purge without the worry of being judged by others.

These reflective mechanisms provide a structure to guide us through our search for guidance from the Holy Spirit. The Bible tells us that the Spirit will teach us and will lead us to all understanding.[72] It also tells us:

> "But God has revealed it to us by his Spirit. The Spirit searches all things, even the deep things of God. For who among men knows the thoughts of a man except the man's spirit within him? In the same way no one knows the thoughts of God except the Spirit of God." (1 Corinthians 2:10–11, NIV)

As we engage with expectancy in devotional reading, prayer, and critical reflection, we receive spiritual insight through the Word of Truth. We need to be spiritually fit if we are to be ready to discern the message and open ourselves to guidance from the Holy Spirit who will help us figure out how to apply that message to daily contemporary living. You will know that the Spirit of Truth has spoken because the insight will be accompanied by a sense of peace.[73] That has been my experience, and it is through such a process that wisdom grows. What we know spiritually often cannot be expressed in words alone. Sometimes it takes a groan, a sway, a song, a shout, a dance, a clap, or a posture of prayer to communicate our thoughts, feelings, and perspectives. Sometimes through use of such mechanisms we can come close to figuring things out. At other times, we just have to trust the leading of the Holy Spirit and rest in the mystery of Almighty God as we are guided by our peace.

End of Chapter Exercises

1. Try your hand at writing a theological reflection.

2. Write a story reconstructing a particularly stressful or particularly fulfilling time in your life.

3. Write a poem of praise, lament, or release.

4. Write a letter to the future generation about the importance of getting in touch with God.

Part II

Devotionals for Healing and Wholeness

If we are already in relatively good shape holistically, we do not need a rigorous workout. Rather, we should engage in particular levels of exercise to establish or maintain equilibrium in our lives. Three levels of fitness are recommended as part of the *Spiritual Renewal* model: daily maintenance, strength and endurance training, and intensive workouts.

Levels of Spiritual Fitness

Daily maintenance is the level of spiritual exercise with which most of us are familiar. It involves reading a daily devotional, perhaps from a periodical or booklets such as the *Upper Room*. Daily maintenance might also entail following the daily lectionary readings widely available on the Internet and through other sources.[74] Staying fit involves devotional activity that takes place during a time of quietness that typically begins with prayer and is followed by scripture reading and meditation, silent contemplation, and reflective journal writing. The session ends with prayer. If you are in need of routine maintenance, fifteen to twenty minutes of devotional time should be sufficient to give you the spiritual exercise you need. Pray about it, and let the Holy Spirit guide you.

Strength training, the next level of spiritual exercise, is based on the premise that from time to time when we look at a problem or issue that confronts us that issue looms like a mountain in our path—huge and insurmountable. When we stop to examine the problem in light of God's spiritual guidance, we are able to keep things in proper perspective—realizing that nothing is too hard for God. Armed with this confidence, we are able to receive the blessings God has for us, if we are spiritually fit.[75] Strength training uses a scripturally based approach to help those seeking healing and wholeness. People who benefit from this level of exercise are those whose peace has been disturbed in some unspecified way. We are not sure of the source of the disruption or why it has occurred. We just have an acute awareness that something has disquieted us and is showing up through a number of indicators, including our thoughts, emotions, behaviors, physiological indicators, and sources of spiritual unrest.

During strength training I suggest that you involve at least one other person in your exercise regimen. That person might be a prayer partner, a spiritual director, a pastor, a faith-based therapist, a medical professional, or another trusted friend in the spiritual family of God. The bottom line is that you might need someone to walk with you on this intensive leg of your journey toward wholeness. In this phase, without a doubt, two heads are better than one.[76] But the major source of insight comes from the Holy Spirit when we are spiritually attuned to receive what God has for us. Strength training enables us to seek guidance from God to help us identify the complex interrelationships among things that are impairing our relationship with God, and with other people. We pray for revelation and continue to alternate between prayer, silent contemplation, and reflective journaling for as long as necessary. After that, we leave it in the hands of God, the ultimate healer and deliverer.

The *fitness workout* provides a rigorous level of exercise geared toward helping us stretch our spiritual muscles. The goal of the fitness workout is to prepare us to endure when troubles come. As with all devotional exercises in this book, fitness training begins with prayer and centering (during which we assume an attitude of expectancy to receive God's inspiration). It also involves systematic gathering and organization of information, silent contemplation, and reflective journaling. Prayerfully, we engage in a series of steps to help us gain insight from scripture. Therefore, the focus of fitness training is often thematic in its approach, and I believe it works best when we have a specific concern to address.

This level of exercise assumes that the Bible represents the living Word that can be applied to our lives in the present day, with inspiration from the Holy Spirit. The approach assumes that the Word of God and the leading of the Holy Spirit will equip each seeker with seeds for answering contemporary questions. The fitness training regimen employs the KWL approach and structures our inquiries around three critical questions: What do we *know*? What do we *want* to know? What did we *learn*? The procedure uses biblical study tools such as a concordance, bible dictionary, and commentaries.

You may need to acquire additional information from other sources. The most potent tools in this level of exercise are prayer and listening with expectancy. Writing down our insights through reflective journaling gives us a record of our ongoing growth and development. Fitness training may involve thirty to sixty minutes of daily quiet reflection. Conducting your research and journaling may require additional time during the week.

Devotionals for Healing and Wholeness

Sometimes the circumstances of life can be overwhelming, causing traumatized women to feel troubled, unfulfilled, and hurt. Many who have experienced trauma have never been helped to overcome their pain. Tragically, many of them do not realize what is happening to them as they grapple with their depression and sadness. They just know that something is disturbing their peace. They continue to navigate the world as broken vessels. What facilitates the healing process among God's children who have been broken and scarred? Devotionals in chapters seven through eleven will help Christian women (and men) who have a need to engage in spiritual healing, to attain wholeness and fulfillment in their lives.

Chapter Seven

Understanding Trauma

Centering

Find a quiet place to relax and be alone for a while. Breathe deeply—inhale and exhale in rhythmic fashion. Gather your mental, physical, and spiritual faculties as you listen with expectancy and invite the Holy Spirit to give you a refreshed perspective.

Prayer

Precious Lord, open my mind and my heart to receive what you have for me. Peel back the layers by your grace so that I may see clearly your will for my life. Amen.

Focus Scripture: 2 Samuel 13: 1–22—Tamar: A Case of Family Violence and Trauma

Scriptural Context

This scripture tells the story of Tamar, a daughter of King David. Tamar is beautiful and her half-brother Amnon falls in love with her. On the advice of a friend, Amnon pretends to be ill and has Tamar bring food to his bedroom so she can feed him. When she arrives, he rapes her. And following the rape his love for her turns into intense contempt. The scripture tells us "In fact, he hated her more than he had loved her" (v 15). Then he sends her away in disgrace. Tamar is distraught and pleads with her brother not to send her away, for sending her away would be a greater wrong than the rape (v 16). Amnon ignores her pleading and calls his personal servant to throw her out and bolt the door behind her. Deeply troubled, Tamar puts ashes on her head and tears her garments, both of which represent acts of despair. She leaves Amnon's quarters, weeping aloud as she went (v 19). When Tamar sees Absalom, he advises her to "be quiet now, my sister; he is your brother. Don't take this thing to heart" (v 20).

We are told that after that, Tamar lived in her brother Absalom's house as a desolate woman. For all practical purposes, after the rape, Tamar is pushed to the margins. She is disgraced, unmarriageable, and isolated in the house of her brother Absalom. David, her father, does nothing to console his daughter; at least there is no account of such compassion in the scripture. Perhaps David's inaction is due to the guilt he feels; he may recognize that the sins of his children could possibly be traced back to his own misconduct with Bathsheba.

Many people who have read this account have asked the question: What happens to Tamar after the rape? Although we are not given specific information, we can speculate based on contemporary application of this scripture. Some people might conclude that Tamar was deeply troubled as the result of the rape and the disgrace to her family. They might conclude that she was frozen in a state of shame, and no doubt traumatized by her predicament.

Focus Questions

After reading the focus scripture, prayerfully consider the following questions.

1. What do you think the writer wants to convey in this text? What is the central idea?

2. What is your understanding of trauma? How do you believe the concept of trauma is applicable to Tamar's situation?

3. What does this scripture reveal about the long-term effect of family violence?

4. In what specific ways can you apply the lessons of this scripture to contemporary Christian life?

5. In what ways, if any, do you perceive the Holy Spirit at work in this scripture?

Silent Contemplation Exercises

During Silent Contemplation find a comfortable place where you can be silent, still, and receptive for several minutes without interruption. Quietly reflect on how you believe the Holy Spirit is guiding you to understand the message of today's scripture. Try to respond to each of the focus questions. Then spend a few minutes recording your thoughts in your journal.

Author's Critical Reflection: Understanding Trauma

Trauma can happen to anyone. When adversity confronts them, people find themselves faced with the ancient survival instincts to fight, flee, or freeze. Fighting and fleeing are liberating responses. Freezing, however, tends to become problematic as we are immobilized by our dread and inability to act. Like a deer blinded by oncoming headlights, we halt abruptly in the middle of the developmental road as we await imminent destruction and watch helplessly as the vehicle of our dread charges toward us. Not having the presence of mind or the tools to elude the impact, we quiver in fear and anticipation of being plowed down in our tracks. We wait. We tremble. We cower. But the impact never comes. In a suspended state we have lost the mind and will to escape. In short, we are traumatized. And until we are able to unfreeze, or to release the pent-up energy we would have expended on fleeing, we are trapped in our terror, and we experience emotional and spiritual pain. Unlike the deer, however, we humans have the capacity to remove ourselves from the path of suffering.

Trauma is a "disordered psychic or behavioral state resulting from mental or emotional stress or physical injury."[77] It is a loss we experience when we have to go without something that we have had and valued or something that we needed, wanted, or expected.[78] In his book, *Walking the Tiger: Healing Trauma*, Peter Levine discusses the traumatic phenomenon:

> "Humans suffer when we are unable to discharge the energy that is locked in by the freezing response...If they are unable to orient and choose between fight and flight, they will freeze or collapse. Those who are able to discharge that energy will be restored. Rather than moving through the freezing response, as animals do routinely, humans often begin a downward spiral characterized by an increasingly debilitating constellation of symptoms. To move through trauma we need quietness, safety, and protection similar to that offered the bird in the gentle warmth of the child's hands. We need support from friends and relatives, as well as from nature. With this support and connection, we can begin to trust and honor the natural process that will bring us to completion and wholeness, and eventually peace."[79]

According to the American Red Cross,[80] in the face of an overwhelming event, people may tend to feel helpless, powerless, and unable to protect themselves. Not everyone has immediate reactions; some reactions are delayed and may show up days, weeks, or even months later. Some people may never have a reaction. A traumatic event can reactivate the emotions associated with previous traumas, which can be overpowering. Trauma occurs when the victim perceives that neither resistance nor escape is possible. The trauma-tized individual may experience intense emotion without clear memories of the event—or may remember every-thing in detail without emotion. Traumatic symptoms have a tendency to become disconnected from their source and to take on a life of their own.

Judith Herman, one of this country's foremost experts on trauma and abuse, describes the impact of trauma.[81] She reports, "small, seemingly insignificant reminders can also evoke these memories, which often return with all the vividness and emotional force of the original event. Thus, even normally safe environments may come to feel dangerous, for the survivor can never be assured that she will not encounter some reminder of the trauma." [82] Children are especially vulnerable because "repeated trauma in childhood forms and deforms the personality." For example, when a child is trapped in an abusive environment and is faced with having to adapt, he or she has to find ways to express their traumatic memories.

Recovery usually happens in three stages: (1) The establishment of safety; (2) remembrance and mourning; and (3) reconnection with ordinary life.

Grieving must occur as a precondition for restoration of a meaningful world. Trauma brings loss; mourning the loss gives the survivor a way to discover her undestroyed strengths and to rebuild her sense of order and justice. Mourning is completed when she reclaims her own history, feels renewed hope and energy for engagement with life. Full recovery is based upon the empowerment of the survivor and the creation of new connections. For Christian women, that empowerment comes from connecting with God through the healing power of Jesus Christ, whose Spirit abides in us. Survivors of chronic childhood abuse face the task of grieving not only what they lost but also for what was never theirs to lose. The childhood that was stolen from them is irreplaceable.

Storytelling as testimony is another step towards healing from trauma. Telling one's story helps to transform the traumatic memory so that it can be integrated into the survivor's life story. The goal of recounting the trauma story is integration. It helps the survivor create a detailed, extensive record of the traumatic experience. By many accounts, the action of telling the story in the safety of a protected relationship can actually produce a change in the processing of the traumatic memory.

Holistic Fitness Exercises

Exercise	Activity
Exercise the Mind	Reflect on a time when your peacefulness was disturbed. Describe the situation. Record your thoughts in your journal.
Exercise the Body	Reflect on how your lack of peacefulness had an impact on you physically. Record your thoughts in your journal.
Exercise the Spirit	Describe how you were able to move from turbulence to peacefulness. How was the Spirit at work in this movement?
Follow Up	While searching the Internet is a good way to get information about a number of topics, you need to be aware that not all sites are equivalent. Do a Google search using the keywords: Understanding Trauma. Locate at least one website that appears to provide valid information. Evaluate the website on the basis of the following questions: What is the purpose of the site? How do you know? Who are the authors or sponsors? Is the information on the site copyrighted? Have experts in the field critiqued the information on the site? How do you know? Is the information biased? What might be indicators of such bias? Record your insights in your journal. (One option you might use for this exercise is the following, which includes attention to the mind, body, and spirit: http://www.tropos.us/understanding%20trauma.htm).

Follow-Up Exercises

Jot down any thoughts, reactions, feelings, and insights that occurred to you while you reflected on the lesson for today. You might want to let these questions guide your journaling.

1. In what ways, if any, did you find reflecting on the scripture helpful?

2. What insights, changes, or new directions have you discerned?

3. In your spare time, use one of the reflective tools (i.e., storytelling, letter writing, theological reflection) to help you make sense of the spiritual insights you gained today.

CREST Activity

If you could have a conversation with Tamar, what would you say to her? Write a letter to Tamar to encourage her and give her support.

Author's CREST

Sweet Baby Girl
© 2008 by Lorrie C. Reed

Sweet baby girl, I never meant to hurt you
So preoccupied was I with my own angst
I neglected to cherish your youth
You grew up too soon
Your eyes saw too much
Your heart carried weight you were never meant to bear

Absent was I when you needed me most
Like a mother, you nurtured me—
For a time I was your child
As you stumbled to discover life's hurtful lessons:
Bury your trust; shield your heart; disguise your pain
Survive by any means necessary

My heart aches for you on those sunny days
When your light barely flickers behind grey-grim clouds
And glimmers of your vibrancy
Shrink behind pillars of brokenness
But I vow to love you fiercely and speak life to your soul
And pray that God will caress you with peace, sweet baby
   girl

Closing Prayer

End your devotional time by communicating with God through prayer. Remember that our prayers don't need to be long, creative, or dramatic. They need only to be sincere. Sometimes the simplest prayers say it all.

Chapter Eight
Sexual Violence

Centering

Find a quiet place where you can relax and be alone. Breathe deeply—inhale and exhale in rhythmic fashion. Gather your mental, physical, and spiritual faculties as you listen with expectancy and invite the Holy Spirit to give you a refreshed perspective.

Prayer

Gracious God, I have stilled and quieted my soul. Speak to me, Lord, as I wait for a word from you. Amen.

Focus Scripture: 2 Samuel 11: 2–5—David, Bathsheba, and Abuse of Power

Scriptural Context

The story of David and Bathsheba illustrates the abuse of power, particularly the sexual power men held over women in David's society. Rape and sexual assault have pervasive effects on the lives it touches and on society in general. Survivors of sexual assault understand its effects. In the context of David's patriarchal world, men routinely exercised such power and privilege, with women assuming role subservience in most situations of everyday life. This included the loss of control over their bodies as sexual beings. It also included their loss of dignity and any accompanying shame that went along with it. Having been summoned to what I am assuming is nonconsensual sex left Bathsheba few options.

Matters are made worse because David is king. For when the king summons a woman to lay with him, her choices become even more limited; she must accede to the king's wishes or suffer the consequences of her disobedience. In far too many respects, the situation is similar today.

Focus Questions

After reading the focus scripture, prayerfully consider the following questions.

1 What do you think the writer wants to convey in this text? What is the central idea?

2 Describe a situation in your life when you have been subjected to abuse of power.

3 What does this scripture reveal about power and control?

4 In what specific ways can you apply the lessons of this scripture to your daily living?

5 In what ways, if any, do you perceive the Holy Spirit at work in this scripture?

Silent Contemplation Exercises

During Silent Contemplation find a comfortable place where you can be silent, still, and receptive for several minutes without interruption. Quietly reflect on how you believe the Holy Spirit is guiding you to understand the message of today's scripture. Try to respond to each of the focus questions. Then spend a few minutes recording your thoughts in your journal.

Author's Critical Reflection: David and Bathsheba—Sexual Abuse

In contemporary terminology, sexual abuse can be described as a situation in which a victim is forced to have sexual intercourse or take part in unwanted sexual activity. Sexual abuse may involve an abuser's coercing the victim to engage in sexual activity by the use of force, guilt, shame, manipulation, or a perceived God-given privilege on the part of the perpetrator. Such abuse always leaves victims with emotional scars. It also reveals the male abuser's tendency to denigrate and objectify the female he violates.

I could not help but note that in the David and Bathsheba story, the point of view is that of a male. This is not surprising. Patriarchal households and traditions were the norm in the ancient Near East. Even in modern-day society, patriarchal attitudes of power and control have led men to exert dominance over women in some cases, and to their abuse and/or violation in other cases.[83] Blame for perpetuation of sexual abuse can be spread to many sources. One such source includes the print and electronic media, in my opinion. Women are represented in the media by words, pictures, stories, and images that portray them in degrading ways. Too often, the media are guilty of presenting women as sex objects and people who have no self-respect. In other cases, the media reinforce the notion that men are inherently aggressive, and women naturally passive, so abuse becomes more likely due to human nature. In our materialistic, commercial society these images and misrepresentations are used to sell objects. Unfortunately, such symbols and images also serve to rob women of their full humanity as beings created in the image of God.

Denigration of women further manifests in several other ways: the abuser showing a lack of dignity and respect toward the woman he violates, the abuser objectifying his female intimate partner, or the abuser treating his female intimate partner like property that he owns—as one might interpret the case in David's situation. David's abuse of Bathsheba also holds legal implications in that David has superior legal status as a royal while Bathsheba, the victim, does not. In the David and Bathsheba story, then, the abuse is about power, privilege, and patriarchy.

I can only surmise that in some respects, the pain associated with sexual violence is unimaginable and distinctly different from that associated with other acts of violence against women and violence in our society in general. Marie Fortune confirms this:

> "Sexual violence is, first and foremost, an act of violence, hatred, and aggression. Whether it is viewed clinically or legally, objectively or subjectively, violence is the common denominator. Like other acts of violence (assault and battery, murder, terrorism), there is harm of and injury to victims. The injuries may be psychological or physical. In acts of sexual violence, usually the injuries are both."[84]

Several resources exist to help pastors understand how sexual violence affects women mentally, physically, and spiritually. For example, in a book entitled *I Will Survive*, Lori Robinson tells the story of the anger, shame, terror, and trauma she suffered when two men pointed a gun to her head and violated her in her apartment in 1995.[85] In her account of the rape, she points out that "sexual victimization can be the catalyst for the mildest to the most severe dysfunctions, such as low self-esteem, substance abuse, and depression."[86] Robinson lived to tell her story and to use it as a vehicle of healing for other women. During her healing process, she was fortunate enough to connect with two female pastors who walked with her on part of her journey. These pastors who accompanied Robinson were deeply spiritual in their approach to counseling. They connected with Robinson's natural inclination to turn to the Holy Spirit for help. Robinson acknowledges that African Americans, as a people, are spiritual by virtue of their cultural roots, which have conditioned them to rely on their relationship with God for sustenance and survival, even in the face of the most reprehensible experiences. Drawing insights from interviews with these two seasoned women of God (who also are survivors of violence) Robinson reported that:

"Healing is a two-way street. Healing is part God's responsibility and part our responsibility. No victim can ever get
rid of the scars. But you can move past that debilitating
hurt and anger and unforgiveness…Some of us who have
been rape victims choose to live lives of desolation. We
choose. Because you don't have to stay in the place that
you're in, because the potter really does want to put us
back together. We were broken to be glued together in a
better way. We were not just broken and dumped."[87]

Robinson's interviews with these pastors emphasized that
healing is a process that takes time and work and communication with supportive others. Such companions may
include family, friends, counselors, pastors, or someone from
the church family.

Holistic Fitness Exercises

Exercise	Activity
Exercise the Mind	Going through a process of critical reflection helps you assimilate or accommodate the new information with guidance from the Holy Spirit—the mind of God. What new information have you encountered in our scripture study for today? Write your responses in your journal.
Exercise the Body	Breathe Deeply: Deep breathing is a basic technique for relaxation. Breathing slowly and deeply can help turn off stress and turn on peaceful feelings. Find a place where you can sit comfortably. Close your eyes. Inhale slowly and deeply through your nose until you have filled your stomach cavity as full as possible. Purse your lips and exhale slowly. Try doing this activity for five minutes.[88]
Exercise the Spirit	Think about a time when information you received about a spiritual matter conflicted with information you already believed to be true. What resources did you use to help you "hold onto the good" information and let go of the bad? What did you do to resolve the conflict? Record your responses in your journal.

Follow-Up Exercises

Jot down any thoughts, reactions, feelings, and insights that occurred to you while you reflected on the lesson for today. You might want to let these questions guide your journaling.

1. In what ways, if any, did you find reflecting on the scripture helpful?

2. What insights, changes, or new directions have you discerned?

3. In your spare time, use one of the reflective tools (i.e., storytelling, letter writing, theological reflection) to help you make sense of the spiritual insights you gained today.

CREST Activity

Write a prayer for women who have been victimized by abuse of power by someone in authority. Record the prayer in your journal.

Author's CREST

Thief
© 2007 by Lorrie C. Reed

You had no right to steal my life
Minding my own business, I was satisfied
To play the child I was entitled to be

Then you stunted my development
Ripped out my joy, disturbed my peace
Truncated my youth and killed my hope

Now as bitter and thankless as you
I am restless in the daytime
Sleepless and fitful in the night

Afraid that I have gone blind
For I can't see my future from here
And I'm terrified to venture into the dark

Closing Prayer

End your devotional time by communicating with God through prayer. Remember that our prayers don't need to be long, creative, or dramatic. They need only to be sincere. Sometimes the simplest prayers say it all.

Chapter Nine
Domestic Violence

Centering

Find a quiet place to relax and be alone for a while. Breathe deeply—inhale and exhale in rhythmic fashion. Gather your mental, physical, and spiritual faculties as you listen with expectancy and invite the Holy Spirit to give you a refreshed perspective.

Prayer

Gracious God, I pray that you extend your mercy to women who have been abused and hurt. Surround them with your love and your healing presence. Amen.

Focus Scripture: Judges 19: 16–30—Violence against a Virgin and a Concubine

Scriptural Context

Domestic violence has been around for a very long time—dating back to antiquity. One of the earliest biblical accounts of violence in the home is documented in Genesis 4 when Cain slays his brother Abel (v 8). Another account describes a man who was traveling with an entourage. Strangers expressed a wish to do harm to those in the group. The leader of the traveling group offered the strangers his virgin daughter and his concubine to appease them. "I will bring them out to you now," said the man, "and you can use them and do to them whatever you wish. But to this man, don't do such a disgraceful thing" (Judges 19:24). Genesis 37 provides another example featuring the sons of Jacob, who are jealous of their brother Joseph: "Come now, let's kill him and throw him into one of these cisterns and say that a ferocious animal devoured him. Then we'll see what comes of his dreams" (v 19-20). In 2 Samuel 13:1–16, the rape of Tamar by her half-brother Amnon is described.

Focus Questions

After reading the focus scripture, prayerfully consider the following questions.

1. What do you think the writer wants to convey in this text? What is the central idea?

2. What do you believe contributes to the perpetuation of domestic violence in biblical times? In the Modern-day?

3. What does this scripture reveal about the causes and effects of domestic violence?

4. In what specific ways can you apply the lessons of this scripture to contemporary Christian life?

5 In what ways, if any, do you perceive the Holy Spirit at work in this scripture?

Silent Contemplation Exercises

During Silent Contemplation find a comfortable place where you can be silent, still, and receptive for several minutes without interruption. Quietly reflect on how you believe the Holy Spirit is guiding you to understand the message of today's scripture. Try to respond to each of the focus questions. Then spend a few minutes recording your thoughts in your journal.

Author's Critical Reflection:
Domestic Violence

The term *domestic violence,* broadly defined, encompasses abuse found in child/child, parent/child, spouse/spouse, partner/partner, adult child/aging parent relationships, as well as violence among siblings and in dating relationships.[89] This social malady constitutes a purposeful pattern of coercive behavior that takes the form of repeated physical, sexual, emotional/psychological, economic, and spiritual abuse tactics. Domestic violence typically takes place in the context of dating, family, or household relationships.[90] According to Miki Paul[91], abuse deprives one of freedom of doing what one wishes; in other cases abuse forces one to behave in ways one does not want to behave. "Domestic violence is simply a show of power by one person over another. Perpetrators choose to demonstrate to their partners that they are in control, no matter what."

Various factors contribute to the perpetuation of domestic violence. Many people have become immune to the tragedy and have grown calloused. They tend to feel that domestic violence is a private matter representing the status quo, and there is nothing any of us can do about it. The tenacity of domestic violence is partially attributable to a three-phase cycle of abuse.[92] This cycle is well-known and has been referred to often in the literature about domestic violence. It represents one framework for analyzing domestic abuse and may not fit all situations. As commonly presented, the cycle of violence includes a number of steps—tension, violence, and contrition, according to Berry and others who have examined the phenomenon.[93]

Another factor contributing to the perpetuation of domestic violence is religion. Leaders in communities of faith often counsel women to stay in an abusive relationship and preserve the marriage at all costs. Beyond that many leaders in communities of faith simply fail to acknowledge that domestic abuse violates the sanctity of life, infringes on human rights, and disregards the fact that abused women, too, were created in the image of God.

Theologians and activists such as Marie Fortune have addressed the issue. Fortune argues that domestic violence is sinful and unjust. When questioned as to why God would allow such suffering among women, Fortune's response places the onus squarely on the shoulders of society, as she challenges the suffering argument with the following:

> "The question for us is not who sinned (in cosmic terms) or how can God allow women to be beaten and raped, but how can *we* allow this to go unchallenged? In challenging this victimization, the question is, who is accountable for this suffering and how can justice be wrought here"?[94]

Fortune contends that we should refuse to endure evil and should seek to transform suffering; in this way we can be about "God's work of making justice and healing brokenness."[95]

This response provides satisfaction for some victims because their "deepest need is to somehow explain this experience, to give it specific meaning in one's particular life. By doing this, victims begin to regain some control over the situation".[96] Gaining control changes the person's status from victim to survivor. Being a survivor means moving from a

> "passive, powerless position of victim in which she expected God to protect her to a more mature and confident position of survivor in which she recognized her strength and responsibility to care for herself with God's help. In addition, her compassion and empathy for others increased and she was empowered to act to change things that cause violence and suffering. She was able to transform her experience and mature in her faith as she recovered from the assault with the support of family and friends."[97]

Other groups endorse a similar view and indicate that faith communities could greatly facilitate the healing of victims of domestic violence through re-introducing them to a God who loves them and does not want them to be injured in any way.[98]

Holistic Fitness Exercises

Exercise	Activity
Exercise the Mind	Use the Internet to find out more information about a social issue that weighs heavily on your heart. Start out by making a list of what you know. Record your thoughts in your journal.
Exercise the Body	Develop a list of questions on what additional information you want to know. Record your thoughts in your journal. Use this list to identify keywords for your Internet search. If you have the chance, visit a shelter for battered women. Or volunteer to serve a few hours at a shelter for the homeless. Write a few paragraphs on what you learned as the result of this exercise. Record your thoughts in your journal.
Exercise the Spirit	Read over your journal entries for this activity. Reflect on any spiritual insights you gained as the result of completing this exercise. Be as specific as possible. Record your thoughts in your journal.

Follow-Up Exercises

Jot down any thoughts, reactions, feelings, and insights that occurred to you while you reflected on the lesson for today. You might want to let these questions guide your journaling.

1. In what ways, if any, did you find reflecting on the scripture helpful?

2. What insights, changes, or new directions have you discerned?

3. In your spare time, use one of the reflective tools (i.e., storytelling, letter writing, theological reflection) to help you make sense of the spiritual insights you gained today.

Crest Activity

Write a poem about domestic violence. It doesn't have to be long, and it doesn't have to rhyme. It should be a heartfelt expression of your reactions to domestic violence you have experienced, observed, or encountered through the media.

Author's CREST

Boundaries
© 2007 by Lorrie C. Reed

I did nothing to provoke you!
Yet you treat me like I'm filth.
You demean, slap, bruise, and kick me,
Put me down, harass, and hurt.

Don't cajole and drive me crazy.
And stop damaging my things!
Cease the spying and the lying,
And the scornfulness it brings!

Can I bear more isolation?
I'm emotionally starved!
Don't control me and don't curse me,
Put me down or do me harm!

Don't you monitor my movements!
There is no need to be cruel!
Find some other way to quench your
Need for power and control!

Closing Prayer

End your devotional time by communicating with God through prayer. Remember that our prayers don't need to be long, creative, or dramatic. They need only to be sincere. Sometimes the simplest prayers say it all.

Chapter Ten

Childhood Witness

Centering

Find a quiet place where you can relax and be alone for a while. Breathe deeply—inhale and exhale in rhythmic fashion. Gather your mental, physical, and spiritual faculties as you listen with expectancy and invite the Holy Spirit to give you a refreshed perspective.

Prayer

All-knowing God, many times I cannot see the larger picture until you reveal it to me. Open my mind, my heart, my eyes, and my ears so I can receive what you have for me today. Amen.

Focus Scripture: Luke 13:10–17—Woman Waiting for Deliverance for 18 Years

Scriptural Context

The focus scripture for this lesson describes a woman who had been crippled for eighteen years. For all that time she had been bent over and was unable to stand up straight. When Jesus saw her, he set her free from her ailment. He laid his hands on her. Immediately she stood up straight and began praising God (v 13). Having witnessed abuse or violence as a child has a crippling effect, for there are some things that young eyes should never see. This includes children who have witnessed domestic violence in their homes. The crippling effects often last for years.

When it comes to domestic violence, the sins of the ancestors are visited on the children to the third and fourth generation, and beyond. Witnessing violence daily often causes a sense of helplessness in the child. Children who witness domestic violence bear permanent psychological and emotional scars. Too often, these children become the next generation of batterers or maladjusted members of society, although not all people who were abused will become abusers. Likewise, not all people who were victimized as children become victims, although men who are perpetrators most likely have been scarred at some point during their formative years. Regardless of the circumstances, children who were abused or who witnessed abuse in the home tend to be diminished by their past experiences.[99] One way to be set free from such bondage is to turn the confusion over to the Lord, the healer and liberator.

Focus Questions

After reading the focus scripture, prayerfully consider the following questions.

1. What do you think the writer wants to convey in this text? What is the central idea?

2. Describe a situation in your life when you thought deliverance would never come.

3. What does this scripture reveal about patience and waiting on the Lord?

4. In what specific ways can you apply the lessons of this scripture to your daily living?

5. In what ways, if any, do you perceive the Holy Spirit at work in this scripture?

Silent Contemplation Exercises

During Silent Contemplation find a comfortable place where you can be silent, still, and receptive for several minutes without interruption. Quietly reflect on how you believe the Holy Spirit is guiding you to understand the message of today's scripture. Try to respond to each of the focus questions. Then spend a few minutes recording your thoughts in your journal.

Author's Critical Reflection: Childhood Witness

According to *Mental Health Today,* children experience trauma as the result of lived or observed experiences:

> "Witnessed events include, but are not limited to, observing the serious injury or unnatural death of another person due to violent assault, accident, war, or disaster or unexpectedly witnessing a dead body or body parts. Events experienced by others that are learned about include, but are not limited to, violent personal assault, serious accident, or serious injury experienced by a family member or a close friend; learning about the sudden, unexpected death of a family member or a close friend; or learning that one's child has a life-threatening disease."[100]

Aside from the effects of witnessing the violence, children of abused mothers often have very little nurturance and support at home because the mother is enmeshed in her own personal struggle to survive which includes pacifying the batterer. This often leaves them with little energy or emotional ability to care for their children. Frequently, children become victims of the violence and suffer emotionally as well as physically along with their mothers. In cases where children do not have abuse directed toward them, the mere witnessing of abuse toward their mother can often cause deep running, long lasting emotional scars that can forever change their lives and their perception of the world. Some of the children who have been exposed to this brand of trauma and violence learn to internalize their feelings, which may lead to self-destructive behaviors, such as misuse of drugs and alcohol, or depression, suicidal thoughts, and social withdrawal or isolation.[101]

The author of this book will never be able to reclaim the 50+ years she spent searching for peace and self-assurance. For most of her life she wandered around in a fog. Never satisfied even when she was a child, she searched constantly for something that was missing in her life. In school she was the overachiever—she had to be the first, the best, and the brightest. Nothing less was good enough. This trend continued as she moved from adolescence into adulthood and on to middle age. Always searching, almost reaching, ever falling short, she longed for that one nameless thing that continued to elude her. She coveted it; she probed for it; she craved it, in spite of the fact that she was never able to give *it* a name or a face. She would know it when she saw it, she kept telling herself. So she searched without ceasing. The quest consumed her and, ironically, became for her the source of great anguish. That's until she met Jesus and learned about the power of unwavering faith.

Through her continual analysis and reflection, she has come to realize that she made a lot of mistakes in her life. She also came to realize that many of the choices she made were pretty much out of her control, for they had been determined by the roles she assumed as the result of her childhood experiences with violence and abuse. Fortunately, her life is not over. She still has many chances to live in a meaningful and satisfying future that is informed by an understanding of her past. So she mourned the years she lost, realizing that she will never get them back. She released her resentment and she let those years rest in peace. As a result, she has an opportunity to move forward armed with hope. Rather than dwelling morbidly on the past, she has turned her attention to making the best of every day of her life that remains. She discovered that in spite of the level of hurt and pain children have experienced in their lives, they are still capable of healing from trauma. Grieving is part of the process. But it also takes faith.

Holistic Fitness Exercises

Exercise	Activity
Exercise the Mind	Place yourself at the scene of your favorite bible story. Assume that you are an onlooker. Recreate the physical scene in your mind with as much detail as possible. Use a bible dictionary if necessary. Write your description in your journal.
Exercise the Body	Using the same Bible story from the previous segment you will now try to exercise your senses. Imagine what you might see, feel, hear, taste, and smell at the scene. Write your impressions in your journal.
Exercise the Spirit	Now try to articulate what your spirit senses about the scene or situation. How do you sense that the Holy Spirit is at work in this scene? Record your responses in your journal.

Follow-Up Exercises

Jot down any thoughts, reactions, feelings, and insights that occurred to you while you reflected on the lesson for today. You might want to let these questions guide your journaling.

1. In what ways, if any, did you find reflecting on the scripture helpful?

2. What insights, changes, or new directions have you discerned?

3. In your spare time, use one of the reflective tools (i.e., storytelling, letter writing, theological reflection) to help you make sense of the spiritual insights you gained today.

CREST Activity

Place yourself in the afflicted woman's shoes. Write the story of her healing from her perspective.

Author's CREST

Childhood Lessons
© 2007 by Lorrie C. Reed

From my hiding place I studied you
Cringing when he lunged
Throwing up your hands
Protecting your head
Through his fits of drunken madness

Even through your tears
You whispered love and endured
Affirming that he was king of the castle
While never claiming your
Rightful place as his queen

Closing Prayer

End your devotional time by communicating with God through prayer. Remember that our prayers don't need to be long, creative, or dramatic. They need only to be sincere. Sometimes the simplest prayers say it all.

Chapter Eleven

Steps in the Healing Process

Centering

Find a quiet place where you can relax and be alone for a while. Breathe deeply—inhale and exhale in rhythmic fashion. Gather your mental, physical, and spiritual faculties as you listen with expectancy and invite the Holy Spirit to give you a refreshed perspective.

Prayer

Awesome God, thank you for sending your Spirit as you breathe into me the healing wind of eternal life. Thank you for second chances. Help me to walk in a way that honors you. Amen.

Focus Scripture: Jesus Calms the Storm: Matthew 8:23–26

Scriptural Context

In this story about nature Jesus' disciples are alarmed by an intense, raging storm that comes up as they are on their way to the other side of the lake. Fearing that they will perish, the disciples awaken Jesus who is asleep at the back of the boat. Jesus chides the disciples because of their lack of faith. Then he rebukes the storm, and there is a perfect calm. The disciples were astonished and wondered what kind of man was this that the winds and seas obeyed him. What a comfort to know that in perilous times, Jesus can speak calm to our stormy circumstances!

Focus Questions

After reading the focus scripture, prayerfully consider the following questions.

1   What do you think the writer wants to convey in this text? What is the central idea?

2   Describe a situation in your life when you felt you were in the middle of a raging storm.

3   What does this scripture reveal about human nature? About Jesus? About peace?

4   In what specific ways can you apply the lessons of this scripture to your daily Christian life?

5   In what ways, if any, do you perceive the Holy Spirit at work in this scripture?

Silent Contemplation Exercises

During Silent Contemplation find a comfortable place where you can be silent, still, and receptive for several minutes without interruption. Quietly reflect on how you believe the Holy Spirit is guiding you to understand the message of today's scripture. Try to respond to each of the focus questions. Then spend a few minutes recording your thoughts in your journal.

Author's Critical Reflection: Peeling Away the Layers

Sometimes the metaphorical storms of life can resemble tightly wound balls with many layers and textures that frighten and disturb us. Even with all that complexity, peace is possible. The author of this book, for example, found peace and healing by placing her trust in Jesus. Her healing involved peeling off the pain layer by layer—identifying specifically those things that weighed her down, examining their impact on her life, casting her cares on the Lord, and then letting go of the hurt, resentment, and bitterness.

With each new revelation came a new release. And with each new release, she could feel herself growing stronger. Only then was she able to move on to the next revelation. And she could feel her faith increase. She worked diligently on her spiritual renewal. Then, miraculously, after about four years of intensive reflective work, she realized that there was nothing left to peel away. All the pain and resentment were gone. She had finally managed to work out the haziness that once blanketed her. Renewed, restored, and reborn, she felt spiritually fit to carry out God's plan for her life. Today, she is healed and at peace with who she is. The shackles had finally been broken, and she was free by the grace of God, the master healer. When equilibrium was restored to her life, she felt as if she had been born again. And in many ways rebirth is precisely what had occurred, a birth mediated by God through the agency of the Holy Spirit. She had learned the fine art of walking with a limp, so to speak, and without a doubt, she still had scars, but both the limp and the scars became almost imperceptible. Some of the steps she engaged in during her healing process are outlined below:

Stop being the victim. The very first step in her healing demanded that she stop being the victim! The Bible tells us that we are slaves to whatever has mastery over us.[102] And she was definitely a slave to low self-esteem and aimlessness. One day, she decided that she was not going to be the victim any more. As long as she let people hurt her, they would keep on doing so. So she decided to get to the bottom of her angst and restore equilibrium in her life. As part of a self-care and spiritual formation routine, she engaged in a daily regimen of prayer, silent reflection, written reflection, scripture reading, and writing poetry, often as a therapeutic activity. On most days her devotionals lasted for two hours or more, for she was in need of intensive spiritual care. These devotional periods served as a time of refreshing, healing, and renewal.

Engage in quiet devotion. Her daily devotional time involved reading the Bible and applying its wisdom to her circumstances. In the stillness and silence, she made herself vulnerable as she searched the Word expectantly for answers to her questions. In such a state of contemplation she was compelled to let go of those things that weighed her down emotionally and spiritually. For her, the daily devotional involved removing obstacles to knowing and loving God. And in the end, God's love prevailed.

Write something every day. She took great pains to get her story straight. So she wrote and rewrote her saga until she was satisfied that she had sorted out the details and made sense of what had occurred in her life. With certain details of her past, for example, she dumped every bit of her pain into a novel. And when she had put the last period on the last sentence, she felt free. The important thing is that after she reconstructed her version of the story, the events of her life no longer had the power to hurt her—whether that hurt had been intentional or not. Her life made sense to her at last, and the effect was liberating.

Do something positive for someone else. As a matter of routine, she began to give a little more of her time and energy to others. Part of her healing involved volunteering to serve on committees, serving meals to the homeless, and working as a rape crisis advocate. She also volunteered to facilitate a long-term Bible study class at her church. With each act of giving she was able to peel away another layer of pain and confusion. But she also remembered to keep some of her time and energy for herself in the process.

Think positive thoughts. She tried to eliminate negativity from her thoughts and vocabulary as much as possible. Every day, she tried to make a conscious effort to live out the advice Paul gave to the Philippians: "whatsoever things are true, whatsoever things are honest, whatsoever things are just, whatsoever things are pure, whatsoever things are lovely, whatsoever things are of good report; if there be any virtue, and if there be any praise, think on these things" (Phil 4:8).

Listen to music. Music had a calming effect on her. It gave her a sense of peace and well-being that she could find from no other source. For her, soft and soulful music or smooth jazz rendered the best effects. So she incorporated smooth gospel and jazz into her daily listening regimen. It made a big difference in her mood and reinforced in her a sense of peace.

Forgive and move on. She discovered that healing was related to forgiveness. She knew that she had been successful at forgiving and moving on when she was able to think about painful things that had affected her life without shedding tears. Her process of forgiveness involved forgiving her father for abusing her mother, for being an angry alcoholic, and for abandoning her at a young age. She had no peace until she was finally able to release him from the hell to which she had relegated him, and she let him rest in peace. After going through these steps, she felt so much stronger and much more confident. This strength was born from her ability to forgive and move on.

Maintain physical health. Attending to her physical health ensured that she had enough strength and stamina to fight for her survival. First, after she decided that she wanted to live, she realized she needed to be in good health to do so productively. That said she visited her doctor for her annual checkups. Her family had a history of high blood pressure, high cholesterol, and obesity. All of these things are interrelated, so she made sure her medications were up to date. She focused on development of good eating habits and lifestyles. All of this has affected her overall sense of well-being. And her physical well-being has, in turn, reinforced her overall sense of mental and spiritual health. In spite of all these remedial steps, she still struggles with her health and her weight. She prays continually about these issues.

Lighten up. She stopped taking life so seriously and found opportunities to engage in laughter and play. The stories of her life had been so sad in the past. She decided to look for the positive things in everything she encountered. She even purchased a "Tickle Me Elmo," the Sesame Street doll that rolls on the floor in a fit of hilarity. His laughter is infectious, and she activated him when she was feeling down. She tried to do those things that made her happy. Today she no longer gives all of herself to others without keeping some of her energy for herself. She has recaptured her joy, and she feels at peace most of the time these days.

Learn about the Issues. She made a deliberate effort to educate herself about those issues that had affected her negatively in the past. She attended workshops, read books and research studies, took classes, and talked to people who were knowledgeable about those things that had such a devastating impact on her life. The more she learned, the more empowered she felt. She surrendered her life to the will of God, and, in doing so was able to deploy that knowledge to intervene in the destructive cycles that had plagued her in the past.

Seek help, when necessary. Soon after she realized the nature of her issues, she knew she wouldn't be able to help anyone until she, herself, had healed to a reasonable extent. Since that time, she has engaged vigorously in "the work" of reaching wholeness. After much prayer, she sought the help of a therapist and of a pastoral counselor, both of whom helped her work through the complexities of her past. As the result of therapy, pastoral counseling, prayer, and reflection, she began to see more clearly where she was headed and why. Her desire was to avoid repeating the mistakes of her past. Soon her issues ceased to overwhelm her.

Holistic Fitness Exercises:

Exercise	Activity
Exercise the Mind	Describe what it means to have peace. How do the mind, body, and spirit figure into the equation? Record your responses in your journal.
Exercise the Body	Rest: A well-rested body is more resistant to stress. Try getting to bed at a reasonable hour, especially if you're under stress. Master the art of getting ready for bed. Do something relaxing before bedtime, such as taking a peaceful walk, a warm bath, a warm drink. Try to let go of the trouble of the day. As you lie down, visualize your body restoring itself with slumber.[103]
Exercise the Spirit	Describe how the mind, body, and spirit might contribute to future feelings of peace and contentment. List a few specific things you need to do to overcome barriers between you and your peace of mind.

Follow-Up Exercises

Jot down any thoughts, reactions, feelings, and insights that occurred to you while you reflected on the lesson for today. You might want to let these questions guide your journaling.

1. In what ways, if any, did you find reflecting on the scripture helpful?

2. What insights, changes, or new directions have you discerned?

3. In your spare time, use one of the reflective tools (i.e. storytelling, letter writing, theological reflection) to help you make sense of the spiritual insights you gained today.

CREST Activity

Write a prayer for the wisdom, courage, and strength to be free of the restrictions you wrote about in this exercise. Record the prayer in your journal.

Author's CREST

After You Prayed, I Prayed
© 2007 by Lorrie C. Reed
November 28, 2007

After you prayed, I prayed
Her pain deserved more than childhood verse—
You know, those little poems you chanted
At Big Mama's knee when she first taught you how to
Talk to the Lord!

Her pain was as deep as the seas
As high as the clouds
As dense as all eternity!
A simple rhyming couplet would never fill the void—
No nursery tune could pack sufficient power

So I stood in the lonesome gap for her
With sighs so deep I ached for her
Beseeched God's love and grace for her
Somehow knowing that God heard us both
And poured out mercy even as we spoke

Closing Prayer

End your devotional time by communicating with God
through prayer. Remember that our prayers don't need to
be long, creative, or dramatic. They need only to be sincere.
Sometimes the simplest prayers say it all.

Part III

Devotionals for Spiritual Fitness

Daily Devotionals and Exercises for Spiritual Fitness

Chapters in this section consist of devotionals and exercises to help you exercise your ability to get in touch with your spiritual side and develop habits of mind that help you restore the balance of mind, body, and spirit. These chapters will systematically guide you to re-conceptualize your thinking in such a way that the new perspective factors in the spiritual dimension. I urge you to complete the exercises in each chapter. By the time you finish, you will have under your belt a set of critical thinking tools, a problem solving skill, and a devotional framework you did not possess before. These tools will help you strengthen your ability to think spiritually and turn to scripture for guidance when you need answers to life's questions.

Chapter Twelve

Quest for Abundant Life

Centering

Find a quiet place where you can relax and be alone for a while. Breathe deeply—inhale and exhale in rhythmic fashion. Gather your mental, physical, and spiritual faculties as you listen with expectancy and invite the Holy Spirit to give you a refreshed perspective.

Prayer

Merciful and loving God, I ask that you open my spiritual ears to hear the voice of the Shepherd and follow him. And I thank you for the promise of abundant life through Jesus who lives in me through the indwelling Holy Spirit. Amen.

Focus Scripture: John 10:1–10

Focus Questions

Consider the following guiding questions.

1. What do I think the writer wants to convey in this text? What is the central idea?

2. What are the modern-day implications of finding pasture?

3. What does it mean to have abundant life?

4. In what specific ways can I apply the lessons of this scripture to my daily living?

5. In what ways, if any, do I perceive the Holy Spirit at work in this scripture?

6. In what ways, if any, does this text suggest a link between mind, body, and spirit?

Silent Contemplation Exercises

During Silent Contemplation find a comfortable place where you can be silent, still, and receptive for several minutes without interruption. Quietly reflect on how you believe the Holy Spirit is guiding you to understand the message of today's scripture. Try to respond to each of the focus questions. Then spend a few minutes recording your thoughts in your journal.

Author's Critical Reflection

From the first three gospels, we know that Jesus often used familiar, common, and down-to-earth objects to teach spiritual lessons. The images of a shepherd, sheep, sheep pen, and a gate would have been very familiar to the disciples and the audience of that day. A sheepfold is an enclosure where shepherds put their sheep for the night. The pen was usually made out of rocks that were piled high to make four walls. Because the pen had no roof, barbed branches were put on the walls to prevent predators from getting in. A porter usually took charge of the sheepfold while the shepherd spent the night in his own home. When the shepherd returned to the sheepfold in the morning, it was his responsibility to gather his sheep and lead them out to pasture. Some of the accounts I have read said that the shepherd would actually lie across the doorway and would use his body to serve as the gate in order to keep out the wolves, lions, and other predators. This gate was the only passageway leading in and out of the pen. So the sheep had no choice but to pass through the gate in order to get to their destination. Anyone who did not pass through the gate was said to be a thief or a robber.

There was something else peculiar about this sheepfold. It was like a big common, community pen. Everybody's sheep were mixed up with everybody else's sheep, and back then, there were no marks or brands to distinguish one sheep from another. In order to gather the sheep that belonged to him, the shepherd would have to call his sheep by name. Sounds like a strange thing to do, doesn't it? But according to at least one source, Near Middle Eastern shepherds in that day knew the names of all their sheep because sheep were like family pets and had names like "Long Ears" and "White Nose."[104] Like any good household companion, the sheep recognized the voice of the shepherd and followed him. The shepherd then would lead the sheep out, walking ahead of them, and talking to them so they could hear his voice.

This passage of scripture has made me examine through new lenses the concepts of pasture and abundant life. I visited a website called textweek.com and read one of the commentaries there. The author of one commentary pointed out that a pasture is a place that has plants that are alive and that are used for nourishment of a flock. The imagery of nourishment has been associated frequently with Jesus. In these accounts, Jesus is giving something tangible to people who are hungry in order to satisfy their need to be fed. This feeding takes place not only in a physical sense, but also in a spiritual sense, as Jesus reveals himself as the bread of life, the only sustenance that is needed.

Abundance is another term I needed to explore. Abundance means that something is very plentiful, more than sufficient, or in rich supply. Abundance is not necessarily a quantitative concept like economic wealth or possession of material goods. Instead, it can also be qualitative in nature and pertain to richness in physical well-being or sufficiency of inner peace. In Jesus' day, Christians did not enjoy abundance. Instead, they experienced on a regular basis, physical persecution and religious uncertainty. They were the masses that were seeking victory over poverty, freedom from disease, acceptance by a hostile government, and simple justice in everyday matters.

Jesus came preaching a message of hope and promising to lead them to abundant and eternal life. In many cases the masses heard his voice and they followed him. This concept of "abundance" applies equally in the modern day. It equates to assurance that comes when Jesus attends to the fragility and vulnerability of life. Abundance equates to comfort of the body and nourishment of the spirit in the face of tremendous odds.

In a modern-day context, sometimes sheep wander into the valleys of oppression and misfortune. Sometimes they experience sad memories and lonely nights. Sometimes the sheep are victimized by crime, violence, apathy, and cynicism that plague our modern world. And often, the sheep are distracted by unfulfilled dreams and broken promises. Because the thief comes to steal their joy, kill their peace, and destroy their hope—they sometimes get confused, stressed out, and cannot find their way back to the pasture. But Jesus is showing us the way, even today—his Word is true and sure and everlasting. If we, the modern-day sheep, listen to his voice and follow him, he will lead us to pasture, he will feed us with the Bread of Life, he will guide us, and he will preserve us by his Spirit that assures a life of abundance in a world of great scarcity. People who are spiritually fit have been conditioned to hear Jesus' voice speaking through the Word with guidance from the Holy Spirit. They trust that voice and follow it.

Author's CREST

What If the Poems Don't Rhyme?
© 2007 by Lorrie C. Reed

Fields of grass with trees and fragrant buds
Cerulean sky with wispy, painted clouds
Round crayon sun suspended high at noon
Father, mother, sister, brother, and a fraction
Life written in couplets with rhyming verse

Play yards swept clear of glass and broken needles
Smog and exhaust, filmy, dim, and colorless
Spears of light spike through gloom on a good day
Family broken, divided, and pawned at your pleasure
So…what if the poems don't rhyme?

Follow-Up Exercises

Jot down any thoughts, reactions, feelings, and insights that occurred to you while you engaged in this Spiritual Renewal process for today. You might want to let these questions guide your journaling.

1. In what ways, if any, did the process of critical reflection resonate with you?

2. As you completed the exercises, did you sense any tension in the equilibrium of your mind, body, and spirit?

3. What insights, changes, or new directions have you discerned?

4. In your spare time, use one of the reflective tools (i.e., storytelling, letter writing, theological reflection) to help you make sense of the spiritual insights you gained today.

Closing Prayer

End your devotional time by communicating with God through prayer. Remember that our prayers don't need to be long, creative, or dramatic. They need only to be sincere. Sometimes the simplest prayers say it all.

Chapter Thirteen

Rebirth and Renewal

Centering

Find a quiet place where you can relax and be alone for a while. Breathe deeply—inhale and exhale in rhythmic fashion. Gather your mental, physical, and spiritual faculties as you listen with expectancy and invite the Holy Spirit to give you a refreshed perspective.

Prayer

Loving God, I am a child in the Spirit, newly born and leaning on you to nourish me. Help me so I can grow in awareness of who you are. Open my mind and heart to receive what you have for me today. Amen.

Focus Scripture: John 3:1–8

Focus Questions

Consider the following guiding questions.

1. What do I think the writer wants to convey in this text? What is the central idea?

2. What is my understanding of the "Kingdom of God"?

3. What does it mean to be "born again" in a modern-day context?

4. In what specific ways can I apply the lessons of this scripture to my daily living?

5. In what ways, if any, do I perceive the Holy Spirit at work in this scripture?

6. In what ways, if any, does this text suggest a link between mind, body, and spirit?

Silent Contemplation Exercises

During Silent Contemplation find a comfortable place where you can be silent, still, and receptive for several minutes without interruption. Quietly reflect on how you believe the Holy Spirit is guiding you to understand the message of today's scripture. Try to respond to each of the focus questions. Then spend a few minutes recording your thoughts in your journal.

Author's Critical Reflection

Today's scripture tells us that in order to enter the Kingdom of God, you must be born again. While I remember hearing these words from the time I was very young, I didn't start to understand their meaning until recently when I began to reflect on the conversation between Jesus and Nicodemus. In this conversation, Jesus explains to Nicodemus that rebirth is both physical and spiritual—in other words, being born again involves being cleansed with water and receiving new life from the Spirit of God. Since the times of the ancient church baptism has served as a rite of initiation into the community of faith. After baptism, Christians are permitted to receive the Eucharist, which puts them in communion with the church and other members of the body of Christ. In another sense, baptism represents a way for Christians to participate in the death and resurrection of Jesus Christ (Romans 6:1–11). In this regard, baptism points to salvation and to the expectation of everlasting life (John 3:16). According to today's text, one must be baptized with water and with the Spirit in order to enter the Kingdom of God. I submit to you that being baptized and being born again are two different phenomena that may or may not occur simultaneously.

Most of us understand readily the use of water in the baptismal rite. John the Baptist made this association for us when he said he came baptizing with water so that Jesus might be revealed to Israel (1:31). For Israel water represents cleansing and purification. But the text tells us that water alone is not enough. One must also be born from above. The Prophet Ezekiel offers some clues as to what this might mean (Ezekiel 36:23–27). God has directed Ezekiel to inform the people they must set themselves apart from idolatrous nations and be initiated into a new nation and a new family of God. Ezekiel tells us that after the cleansing the person will have a "new heart" and a "new spirit" (v 26). Although the presence of the Spirit is mentioned here briefly, it is described in detail in the next chapter of Ezekiel, where the Prophet has a vision in the valley of dry bones (Ezekiel 37:4–6). God tells Ezekiel to:

> "Prophesy to these bones and say to them, 'Dry bones, hear the word of the Lord! This is what the Sovereign Lord says to these bones: I will make breath enter you, and you will come to life. I will attach tendons to you and make flesh come upon you and cover you with skin; I will put breath in you, and you will come to life. Then you will know that I am the Lord.'" (Ezekiel 37:4–6)

Thus, the dry bones have been given new life with a breath from above, along with a change in behavior and a change in outlook, both of which are initiated by God and not by them.

But you might ask: How might this change in outlook play out in the modern day? I can illustrate this by sharing the story of Janis, who has described her baptism experience. After being moved by lively preaching and answering an altar call, Janis was taken to a dressing room where she disrobed and donned a white cap, a white robe, and white slippers. Then she was ushered to the waiting area. She stood there on the platform, awaiting her turn. Finally, someone took her by the elbow and guided her into the warm water. "I baptize you, my sister…" a deacon began to speak. Janis took a deep

breath and was submerged. She reported feeling the sensation of being buried and wondered how long she could hold
her breath. As she emerged and her head parted the surface
of the water, she gulped deeply—her first breath as a new
creation. She reported that immediately she felt light and
free. The change was instant. Stepping out of the water, she
felt that somehow she had been liberated from her former
worries. She felt brand new. Consequently she knew on some
deep level that she would change her behavior and adjust her
outlook from that point forward.

Janis' account may or may not be representative of all
baptisms. And the account may not be typical of everyone
who has received the "baptism of the Holy Spirit." But it does
represent a departure from an old way of life and an arrival
at a new way of viewing the world and acting in the world.
This account describes a symbolic death and resurrection.
Janis was reborn through water and in Spirit. The breath of
life was breathed into her dry bones. In this account, Janis
was "born again."

Author's CREST

Just Say Yes
© 2007 by Lorrie C. Reed
Inspired by Rev 3:20

You knocked softly at the
Back door of my brokenness
You whispered my name
And made me consider you,
With your arms outstretched
And the cure for what ailed me
Resting, like an invitation,
In the palms of your wounded hands!

Follow me, you said quietly.
And I just said, yes!

Follow-Up Exercises

Jot down any thoughts, reactions, feelings, and insights that occurred to you while you engaged in this Spiritual Renewal process for today. You might want to let these questions guide your journaling.

1. In what ways, if any, did the process of critical reflection resonate with you?

2. As you completed the exercises, did you sense any tension in the equilibrium of your mind, body, and spirit?

3. What insights, changes, or new directions have you discerned?

4. In your spare time, use one of the reflective tools (i.e., storytelling, letter writing, theological reflection) to help you make sense of the spiritual insights you gained today.

Closing Prayer

End your devotional time by communicating with God through prayer. Remember that our prayers don't need to be long, creative, or dramatic. They need only to be sincere. Sometimes the simplest prayers say it all.

Chapter Fourteen
Receiving Your Sight

Centering

Find a quiet place where you can relax and be alone for a while. Breathe deeply—inhale and exhale in rhythmic fashion. Gather your mental, physical, and spiritual faculties as you listen with expectancy and invite the Holy Spirit to give you a refreshed perspective.

Prayer

Gracious God, I thank you for new vision. Help me to press my faith into action as I live and move and breathe by your grace. Give me strength and courage to stand up for you in this fickle world. In your Holy Name I pray, Amen.

Focus Scripture: Luke 18:35–43

Focus Questions

Consider the following guiding questions.

1. What do I think the writer wants to convey in this text? What is the central idea?

2. What does this scripture reveal about the blind man? What does it reveal about Jesus?

3. What does it mean to be "called over" by Jesus in a modern-day context?

4. In what specific ways can I apply the lessons of this scripture to my daily living?

5. In what ways, if any, do I perceive the Holy Spirit at work in this scripture?

6. In what ways, if any, does this text suggest a link between mind, body, and spirit?

Silent Contemplation Exercises

During Silent Contemplation find a comfortable place where you can be silent, still, and receptive for several minutes without interruption. Quietly reflect on how you believe the Holy Spirit is guiding you to understand the message of today's scripture. Try to respond to each of the focus questions. Then spend a few minutes recording your thoughts in your journal.

Author's Critical Reflection

In Luke's story, Jesus is making his way from Galilee to Jericho, a city not too far from Jerusalem. Along the way, a blind beggar is sitting on the side of the road. Because the man was blind, he was not able to earn his keep, so he resorted to begging for his livelihood. Poor, disabled, and needy, he was a member of the lowest class in the society of his day. While he was sitting there, the blind man heard the roar of the crowd increase in volume and fervor. Curious about the commotion, the blind man asked what was happening. The crowd told him that Jesus of Nazareth was passing by. Although the man was blind and had to rely on the crowd to interpret the scene for him, he didn't have to ask who Jesus was. He had probably heard many rumors about this man from Galilee. Jesus' reputation had preceded him. Jesus was known for healing the sick, casting out demons, feeding the hungry, making the lame walk, and giving sight to the blind. This Jesus was a healer; that bit of knowledge was all the blind man needed to spring into action.

He began to call out loudly. "Jesus, son of David, have mercy on me!" When the crowd tried to dissuade him, he shouted all the more: "Mercy," he cried out. Jesus approached, hearing the man's cry. Jesus stopped and told his followers to "call him over," asking that the man be brought to him. There was a brief interchange between them: Jesus asked, "What do you want me to do for you?" The blind man replied, "Lord, I just want to see."

The blind man had faith. He believed that Jesus could heal him; Jesus would free him of his wretchedness, and would relieve him of his distress. With new sight, the blind man could have new life and new possibilities. So the blind man persisted, and his persistence paid off. Jesus simply spoke the words:

"Receive your sight." Jesus said. "Your faith has healed you."

The text tells us that after the healing the blind man followed Jesus and became one of Jesus' disciples.

Back in the 1980s there was a movement afoot called "multicultural education." The goal of the movement was to broaden people's perspectives about culture in order to make them understand that there was more than one right way to view the world. One of the tools used by workshop presenters was the picture of a woman. If you looked at the picture from one point of view, you saw an older lady with a large nose and a wrinkled face. Participants in the workshop were asked to continue looking at the picture to see if they could glimpse anything else in the image. As they persisted in staring at the picture some of them had an "aha!" moment. They reported seeing the visage of a much younger woman who was wearing a stylish hat. Her face was turned to the side in a silhouette. Those who watched as the old woman transformed into a young woman had "received new sight," so to speak. But the funny thing about their new perspective was that once the switch had been made, they were never again able to look at the picture without seeing both women. I wonder if this is what happened to the blind man after he "received his sight" on the road to Jericho. Have you received your sight? If so, what are you prepared to do with your new vision?

Author's CREST

Abide with Me
© 2008 by Lorrie C. Reed

I arranged things as you like them
Dusted places hard to reach
Opened windows; let in breezes
Swept behind and under things

Come, abide within my household
Small and humble, meek and low—
Enter—share your holy presence
'Til it's time for us to go

Follow-Up Exercises

Jot down any thoughts, reactions, feelings, and insights that occurred to you while you engaged in this Spiritual Renewal process for today. You might want to let these questions guide your journaling.

1. In what ways, if any, did the process of critical reflection resonate with you?

2. As you completed the exercises, did you sense any tension in the equilibrium of your mind, body, and spirit?

3. What insights, changes, or new directions have you discerned?

4. In your spare time, use one of the reflective tools (i.e., storytelling, letter writing, theological reflection) to help you make sense of the spiritual insights you gained today.

Closing Prayer

End your devotional time by communicating with God through prayer. Remember that our prayers don't need to be long, creative, or dramatic. They need only to be sincere. Sometimes the simplest prayers say it all.

Chapter Fifteen

The Rest of the Story

Centering

Find a quiet place where you can relax and be alone for a while. Breathe deeply—inhale and exhale in rhythmic fashion. Gather your mental, physical, and spiritual faculties as you listen with expectancy and invite the Holy Spirit to give you a refreshed perspective.

Prayer

Gracious God, thank you for sending me the Holy Spirit to help me fill in the gaps. Help me to be spiritually fit so that in the face of uncertainty I can turn to your indwelling presence to guide me. Amen.

Focus Scripture: Luke 24:13–35

Focus Questions

Consider the following guiding questions.

1   What do I think the writer wants to convey in this text? What is the central idea?

2   What does this scripture tell me about people? What does it tell me about Jesus?

3   What does it mean to "recognize Jesus" in a modern-day context?

4   In what specific ways can I apply the lessons of this scripture to my daily living?

5   In what ways, if any, do I perceive the Holy Spirit at work in this scripture?

6   In what ways, if any, does this text suggest a link between mind, body, and spirit?

Silent Contemplation Exercises

During Silent Contemplation find a comfortable place where you can be silent, still, and receptive for several minutes without interruption. Quietly reflect on how you believe the Holy Spirit is guiding you to understand the message of today's scripture. Try to respond to each of the focus questions. Then spend a few minutes recording your thoughts in your journal.

Author's Critical Reflection

I imagine that as the two witnesses were walking and talking, they were trying to connect all the pieces and logically account for all the mind-boggling details pertaining to the recent life, death, and resurrection of Jesus Christ. I can imagine that just as the two witnesses were at the height of their perplexity, a stranger approached and walked along with them. Now this stranger was Jesus, but the witnesses didn't recognize him. Although their eyes saw Jesus, their spirits did not yet know him. As Jesus joined them on the road to Emmaus, their eyes were prevented from grasping who Jesus was. Jesus was just another stranger to them, for they did not yet understand the significance of his presence. As they continued to walk, Jesus asked them what they were discussing. The witnesses were amazed that this stranger was unaware of the extraordinary events that had occurred only days before. They told Jesus their version of the story, as they understood it at that time. But their version of the story only scratched the surface, even as it attempted to fill in the gaps with the sketchy information they had.

Perhaps some of you remember Paul Harvey, a radio news commentator who had a very popular ABC radio show in the 1970s and 1980s called "The Rest of the Story." The premise of the show was that much of what we hear over the airwaves or read in the newspapers is not complete. Paul Harvey was like the roving reporter who attempted to provide additional information to complete the picture—those little details, those forgotten fragments, or those obscure facts that bring the story to life.

On the road to Emmaus that day, perhaps this is the role that Jesus assumed. The witnesses had part of the information, but certainly not all of it. Jesus helped them to reorganize their data and to look at the available information in a different light. In fact, Jesus gave the witnesses a whole different dimension to consider. Jesus told them the "Rest of the Story." I can imagine Jesus saying: "Here's the big picture and here's the evidence I have to back it up. But there are some other things you will just have to take on faith. It will all be revealed in time. Be patient." Oh, what a grand conversation that must have been!

They approached the village. When the travelers in Luke's account reached Emmaus, they invited Jesus to stay with them and to share in the hospitality. Jesus accepted their invitation. When he was at the table with them he "took bread, gave thanks, broke it and began to give it to them" (v 30). Only in the context of hospitality and breaking of bread did they receive their sight. Then, and only then, were their eyes opened, and they recognized Jesus.

With its complex layers and many dimensions, there is more to life than meets the eye. This became clear to me in 2007 on the day the shootings took place at Northern Illinois University. I followed the story as the events were unfolding and as people were trying to make sense of what had happened. The eyewitness news team was on the scene conducting interviews with passersby. Reporters were trying to amass evidence to support theories of what had occurred and why. The one thing that struck me through all this was that the stories told by the eyewitnesses were so different. And I thought to myself as I listened, "Were these people seeing the same thing?"

How reliable are eyewitnesses, anyway? Recently a number of studies have been conducted on human memory. At least one of these studies was conducted in the mid-1970s by Elizabeth Loftus. In her study, participants were shown a slide of a car at an intersection with either a yield sign or a stop sign. When talking to participants about the incident, experimenters introduced false terms into the descriptions, terms that were at odds with what had actually taken place. Results of the experiment showed that participants remembered seeing the false image that was introduced by the experimenters, rather than the true image. The introduction of false cues altered the subjects' memories.

Today's scripture lesson addresses faulty memories to a certain extent. Shortly after the crucifixion of Jesus, two witnesses were traveling to a village called Emmaus, which was about seven miles from Jerusalem. I imagine they were grappling with the details and trying to make sense of the events that had recently occurred. Perhaps they had been eyewitnesses. Or maybe they had gotten their information secondhand. The scripture is not clear on this point. But we can probably surmise that, as the two travelers talked, there were inevitable gaps in their information that needed to be filled in.

Psychologists have long recognized that gap filling and reliance on assumptions are necessary if people are to function effectively in our society. For example, we make assumptions that certain things will occur so that our lives will be ordered and predictable. In another example, when static interferes with a TV or radio broadcast, we may not hear every word, but we fill in the gaps and are able to grasp the gist of the message, nonetheless. Jesus filled in the gaps for the travelers that day, and they were left with the strong desire to go out and tell somebody what they had discerned! Thinking about all this makes me wonder what could happen if today's witnesses could find a way to apply the lessons of Emmaus to contemporary problem solving. I submit to you that we need the Holy Spirit to help us see the rest of the story.

Author's CREST

The Shepherd
© 2008 by Lorrie C. Reed
Dedicated to domestic violence survivors 3/10/2008

The shepherd of my damnation
The man who claims to love me
Stealing my hopefulness
Shining darkness into my twilight
Dragging me through the quagmire
With rod, he prods me toward his will

The ewe, I am, who believes the lie
The one who recoils when he beckons
Cascading into troubled waters
Swirling into despondency and woe
Following without sight or compass
The one who, himself, has lost his way

***

The Shepherd of my salvation
The God who claims to love me, now
Answering my cry in the valley of death
Applying the rod and staff for my comfort
Refreshing me beside still waters
In fields of life, he restores my depleted soul

The Lord of goodness and of grace
The One who truly loves me
Anointing my head with healing oil
Mending my broken heart
Feeding me 'til I want no more
In the Shepherd's house I will dwell forever

Follow-Up Exercises

Jot down any thoughts, reactions, feelings, and insights that occurred to you while you engaged in this Spiritual Renewal process for today. You might want to let these questions guide your journaling.

1. In what ways, if any, did the process of critical reflection resonate with you?

2. As you completed the exercises, did you sense any tension in the equilibrium of your mind, body, and spirit?

3. What insights, changes, or new directions have you personally discerned?

4. In your spare time, use one of the reflective tools (i.e., storytelling, letter writing, theological reflection) to help you make sense of the spiritual insights you gained today.

Closing Prayer

End your devotional time by communicating with God through prayer. Remember that our prayers don't need to be long, creative, or dramatic. They need only to be sincere. Sometimes the simplest prayers say it all.

Chapter Sixteen

Praise as Communication

Centering

Find a quiet place where you can relax and be alone for a while. Breathe deeply—inhale and exhale in rhythmic fashion. Gather your mental, physical, and spiritual faculties as you listen with expectancy and invite the Holy Spirit to give you a refreshed perspective.

Prayer

Thank you, God, for your mercy and for surrounding me with love. Grant me your peace as I wait for a word from you, Amen.

Focus Scripture: Psalm 96:3, 11–12

Focus Questions

Consider the following guiding questions.

1. What do I think the writer wants to convey in this text? What is the central idea?

2. What are some of the specific ways I communicate with God?

3. What are the implications of having a new song in a modern-day context?

4. In what specific ways can I apply the lessons of this scripture to my daily living?

5. In what ways, if any, do I perceive the Holy Spirit at work in this scripture?

6. In what ways, if any, does this text suggest a link between mind, body, and spirit?

Silent Contemplation Exercises

During Silent Contemplation find a comfortable place where you can be silent, still, and receptive for several minutes without interruption. Quietly reflect on how you believe the Holy Spirit is guiding you to understand the message of today's scripture. Try to respond to each of the focus questions. Then spend a few minutes recording your thoughts in your journal.

Author's Critical Reflection

God communicates with us through the music of nature. Through the majesty and exquisiteness of nature, God touches us in indescribable ways. Music also represents a way for God to be in touch with us. We communicate back to God through music and through prayer. And often, it is through music that God answers us and delivers us from our afflictions. Today's scripture attests to God's communication with us:

> "Let the heavens rejoice, let the earth be glad; let the sea resound, and all that is in it; let the fields be jubilant, and everything in them. Then all the trees of the forest will sing for joy; they will sing before the Lord."

The scripture tells us that "Great is the Lord and most worthy of praise" (v 4)! The whole earth should rejoice because Christ is coming to claim his own (v 13).

As I was standing in my kitchen listening to news on the radio, I heard a variety of grim reports. All depressing. All sad. The only thought I could think was "Have mercy, God."

When the news was over, a song began to play. The lyrics went something like this: "There's a day we all face that depletes our strength, and our hearts can hold no more weight. When the source of our faith is not sure anymore, nothing left to do or to say...Have no fear. God's in control. God has the last say so!" I broke out in a smile, and my spirit soared. God, indeed, has the last say. I received that encouragement from music. That morning I was blessed by a "Song in the Key of God." I believe we should praise God through our grief, praise God through our gladness, and praise God through our gratitude.

Thomas A. Dorsey understood this when he wrote "Precious Lord," a song in which he praised God through his grief. Throughout his early years Dorsey felt torn between the sacred and the secular. Filled with wanderlust, young Dorsey left Georgia as part of the Great Migration from the south to the north. When he settled in Chicago, his schedule was hectic and his lifestyle unhealthy. He soon suffered a nervous breakdown at the age of 21. After undergoing a spiritual transformation, however, Dorsey recovered from his condition a few years later and turned his attention exclusively to sacred music. Then tragedy struck.

One evening while he was playing at a revival in St. Louis, he received a telegram informing him that his wife had died in childbirth and that their child had died soon after. Consumed by grief, the young artist stopped writing for a while, reporting that he felt he had been abandoned by God. One night, a friend visited Dorsey and arranged for him to be left alone in a music room with a piano. He spent some time in the solitude of that room. And after a while, Dorsey recalls feeling at peace: And I quote:

> "I felt as though I could reach out and touch God. I found myself playing a melody, one I'd never heard or played before, and words [for "Precious Lord"] came into my head—they just seemed to fall into place."

Today, Thomas Dorsey's "Precious Lord" has been called "the greatest gospel song of all time." For so many people, including myself, the song expresses a profound message of hope and faith. You remember how it goes, don't you?

> Precious Lord, take my hand,
> Lead me on, let me stand,
> I am tired, I am weak, I am worn.
> Through the storm, through the night,
> Lead me on to the light.
> Take my hand, precious Lord,
> Lead me home.

"Songs in the Key of God"—not only should we praise God through our grief, but we also should praise God through our gladness. Ludwig von Beethoven and Henry Van Dyke could attest to this. Beethoven (1815–1827) lived a troubled personal life and started to lose his hearing when he was about 28 years of age. He was often depressed and from time to time contemplated suicide. Many people who appreciate Beethoven's music have said that they perceive echoes of the man's life in the movements of the man's music. His was a life of struggle followed by triumph. Beethoven's 9th Symphony is considered to be one of the composer's greatest accomplishments.

Later, Beethoven's music was combined with lyrics written by poet and preacher Henry J. Van Dyke (1852–1933). The resulting hymn was entitled "Joyful, Joyful, We Adore Thee" and was first published in the Presbyterian Hymnal in 1911. Again, this hymn expresses trust and joy and hope. You know the words, don't you?

> Joyful, joyful, we adore Thee, God of glory, Lord of love;
> Hearts unfold like flowers before Thee, opening to the
>   sun above.
> Melt the clouds of sin and sadness; drive the dark of
>   doubt away;
> Giver of immortal gladness, fill us with the light of day!

"Songs in the Key of God"—we've seen so far that we should praise God through our grief and through our gladness, but we should also praise God through our gratitude. Horatio Spafford (1828–1888) understood this when he wrote "It Is Well with My Soul," a song that grew out of his reaction to a personal tragedy. His four daughters were killed in a collision with another ship at sea. Spafford's wife, alone, survived. Deeply touched by God's mercy, Spafford was able to say, "It is well with my soul." Coincidentally, this song also represents my personal testimony.

There was a time in my life when I was in a perpetual state of sadness as I kept searching for that thing that would make me feel fulfilled. Although I moved from job to job and amassed a variety of degrees, I still felt no sense of peace in my life. Then I discerned a calling to do God's work. So, in 2004, I enrolled in seminary. That first October, a classmate of mine invited me to attend a Domestic Violence Awareness program at his church. I had not planned to attend such a program; in fact, I had never been to such a program before. But I felt compelled to attend this one. The speakers that night captivated me.

I listened to these women tell their stories and had an epiphany. Their story was my mother's story. And in many ways their words contained elements of my own personal journey. As a young child I had been a witness to domestic violence and had suffered through other experiences that had traumatized me. From an early age these experiences affected me, causing me to make choices that minimized my hurt and maximized my survival. But it wasn't until that very night, at my classmate's church, that I was able to name one source of my pain. That's when it got real. Then, and only then, was my recovery able to begin. I am happy to say today, that I am healed! I am brand new! I am at peace with myself and at peace with my past! Today I can declare with conviction that "It is well with my soul!" It is well with my soul!

When peace, like a river, attendeth my way,
When sorrows like sea billows roll;
Whatever my lot, Thou has taught me to say,
It is well; it is well, with my soul.

Author's CREST

"Songs in the Key of G"
© 2007 by Lorrie C. Reed

Gracious God, you have composed for me a symphony.
It sings of your greatness, your goodness, and your glory.
In my pain, I walked beside troubled waters as I listened
    for your voice.
With gentleness you told me to "Be still."
So I laid down my burdens in a green pasture. I released
    my cares to you.
In the verdant valley I opened my soul to your song of
    love.
Through the trees and the breeze you whispered hope;
Through the cicadas and the sparrows you sang of
    healing;
        Through the rippling stream and the rustling
    leaves
You spoke peace to my soul.
Like a masterful musician,
You played your chorus of creation for my listening
    pleasure.
        You met my grief with your grace.
In quietude and solitude I listened—all the while struck,
    grateful,
Awed, and humbled in your presence.
I heard you, God. And I answered.
And today, all is well with my soul!
Praise the Lord! All is well with my soul! Amen.

Follow-Up Exercises

Jot down any thoughts, reactions, feelings, and insights that occurred to you while you engaged in this Spiritual Renewal process for today. You might want to let these questions guide your journaling.

1. In what ways, if any, did the process of critical reflection resonate with you?

2. As you completed the exercises, did you sense any tension in the equilibrium of your mind, body, and spirit?

3. What insights, changes, or new directions have you discerned?

4. In your spare time, use one of the reflective tools (i.e. storytelling, letter writing, theological reflection) to help you make sense of the spiritual insights you gained today.

Closing Prayer

End your devotional time by communicating with God through prayer. Remember that our prayers don't need to be long, creative, or dramatic. They need only to be sincere. Sometimes the simplest prayers say it all.

Chapter Seventeen

Rhythms of Our Lives

Centering

Find a quiet place where you can relax and be alone for a while. Breathe deeply—inhale and exhale in rhythmic fashion. Gather your mental, physical, and spiritual faculties as you listen with expectancy and invite the Holy Spirit to give you a refreshed perspective.

Prayer

Almighty God, you are the Author of all Seasons and the Composer of this symphony called life. You orchestrate the rhythms of time by your Spirit and bring the movements of my life to full and rich resolution. Send me a Word of Truth today. Amen.

Focus Scripture: Ecclesiastes 3:1–8

Focus Questions

Consider the following guiding questions.

1. What do I think the writer wants to convey in this text? What is the central idea?

2. What is my understanding of "seasons" of our lives?

3. What does this scripture reveal about God?

4. In what specific ways can I apply the lessons of this scripture to my daily living?

5. In what ways, if any, do I perceive the Holy Spirit at work in this scripture?

6. In what ways, if any, does this text suggest a link between mind, body, and spirit?

Silent Contemplation Exercises

During Silent Contemplation find a comfortable place where you can be silent, still, and receptive for several minutes without interruption. Quietly reflect on how you believe the Holy Spirit is guiding you to understand the message of today's scripture. Try to respond to each of the focus questions. Then spend a few minutes recording your thoughts in your journal.

Author's Critical Reflection

This has always been one of my favorite passages of scripture. It describes the totality and fullness of these lives we lead. Whenever I read this text it evokes the image of music. A time to dance, a time to mourn, a time to laugh, and a time to heal—all of these things are associated with songs in my life. And when I look at them altogether, they represent the rhythms of our lives. We live our lives in movements, similar to those orchestrated in a symphony. There's a little concordance, a little dissonance, some major tones, and some minor ones. There is both harmony and disharmony. There are variations in rhythm and movement to make the music happy, sad, or soul stirring. To everything *there is* a season, a time for every purpose under heaven—a time to love, a time to hate, a time to mourn, a time to heal. To everything there is music and a rhythm for every purpose under heaven. And when the end of the piece is reached, if it has been masterfully composed, everything is resolved and we have no regrets, for the whole experience has been greater than the sum of its parts.

Not too long ago I attended the homegoing service of a family friend. This service was a celebration in honor of a man who was over 90 years of age and had lived a fruitful life. When people were asked to make remarks, one of his daughters recalled that her dad had said he was satisfied with his life and that he had no regrets. Now this man had been a prominent figure in a number of circles throughout his long life. He had been in a position to make weighty decisions. He had seen both joys and sorrows. He was human, so he had made more than a few mistakes in his life. Yet at the end of his days, he reported that he had no regrets. How does one do that? How does one live a full life and have no regrets at the end of it? I think today's scripture might hold the thread of an answer.

I have always loved music. My mother made me take piano lessons when I was young. And I played the clarinet for many years. In fact, my old clarinet is tucked away in a trunk in a storage unit somewhere. I don't play it any more. But I hold onto it because it represents the rhythms of my life. One of my cousins also took piano lessons, although he was some- what of a prodigy, being able to read music and play by ear. Music became a very important part of my life and a very important part of his.

I remember back in the 1960s—the age of Broadway musical theater. I loved the musical "Camelot." One of my favorite songs from that musical was "If Ever I Would Leave You." Lancelot was promising never to leave Guinevere. At the time, I was very young and didn't think much about such a promise. Later on in the 1960s Burt Bacharach and Hal David were writing prolifically. And Dionne Warwick was recording their music. "As Long as He Needs Me," "A House Is Not a Home," and "Alfie" were a few of my favorites from these artists.

My cousin Manny and I practiced these songs for hours. He would play the songs and I would sing. It was easy for the time to get away from us because we both loved the music. We put together a fairly decent musical repertoire and were invited to many Baptist Missionary Society Fundraising Teas to perform our music. We were always well received.

Whenever I think of those days, the old memories bubble to the surface in vivid color and sound along with the emotions that were stamped on my heart as Manny played and I sang. We had our music and our trust in God. And we believed in the music and the promises it held. Back then we had no regrets as time moved on in sync with the rhythms of our lives, in tune with the harmonies of our existence.

I remember the year 1968. It was a time to mourn and to express hatred of injustice and intolerance. The songs we sang in those days spoke of protest, hope, and freedom as we stood in solidarity with our brothers and sisters who aspired to see brighter days ahead. Those were the days when the people with the loudest voices were silenced by assassinations—voices like Robert Kennedy and Martin Luther King, Jr. Those were the days when songs like "We Shall Overcome" and "Let there be Peace on Earth" tugged at our heartstrings. Although these songs were made popular in the 1950s they took on new significance in the wake of the late 1960s. Hymns like "I Need Thee Every Hour" and spirituals like "Steal Away" also took on special meaning for me.

Then came the 1970s—it was a time for war, a time to break down and build up. For me, the war that affected my life the most was the Vietnam War. For others it may have been World War I, World War II, the Korean War, one of the Gulf Wars, or some other conflict in which humankind has been engaged throughout history. It seems that during times of war, I embraced my faith more closely. I began to reflect on the meaning of life and death, salvation and eternity. Manny and I had lost touch with each other by then, but often I would hear a song I wanted to sing and wish that my cousin Manny were there to play it for me. He always knew how to bring out the best in me, helping me to transport my anger and fear to a crescendo, and then release it in peaceful resolution. He knew how to strike that chord that touched me deeply as it soothed, comforted, and reassured me that everything would be all right one day.

Manny died from complications of HIV/AIDS in the 1990s. But he will never be forgotten because I carry his music in my heart along with my own. Not a day goes by when I don't hear a song that reminds me of him. Several decades have passed since those days when the rhythms and harmony of Manny's life blended perfectly with the melodies of my own. His music lives on. For comfort. For pleasure. Sometimes for disquietude.

Since Manny's death, God has placed many other songs in my life that have taken up residence in various locations in my soul. That music has a way of nestling comfortably in the deep recesses of my inner sanctuary. It surrounds itself with colors, tones, fragrances, emotions, and other images. There the music snuggles for a season—maybe more—wrapped in a big old blanket of memories until it is time for it to be retrieved.

To everything there is a season—a time for every purpose, under heaven. To everything there is music and a rhythm for every purpose, under heaven. Some of that music reminds me of times of love and some of hate. Throughout my life, I have associated certain songs with birth and other songs with death. Certain songs make me weep and others make me laugh. Some songs make me want to dance, and others make me want to sit still and contemplate the deep things of life. Some songs I've associated with times of healing. Other songs I've associated with times of peace.

In my life, as in yours, there has been some concordance as well as some dissonance. There have been some major keys that have clashed for a time with the minor keys of your life. The rhythms and movements have varied, sometimes drastically; they've taken you up and down and back and forth. They've led you down a certain path only to pull you back by way of another. But when all was said and done, the music has been resolved and is still being resolved.

At those times when I have the luxury of sitting back and letting all the rhythms of my life flood over me, what I hear is a beautiful symphony orchestrated by God, the Masterful Maker of the Music. The composition that represents my life is so rich and complex, so intricate and so full that the whole is truly greater than the sum of its various rhythms and movements. To everything *there is* a season—a time for every purpose under heaven. To everything there is music and a rhythm for every purpose under heaven. And when all is said and done, in spite of or maybe even because of all that has happened in my life, I will be able to reach the end of that great symphony we call life, the life that was composed by God, and say with confidence I have no regrets. Praise God! All has been resolved. I have no regrets.

Author's CREST

Devotion
© 2008 Lorrie C. Reed

In stillness of the peaceful morn
Before light pushes back the dark
When dewdrops kiss awakening buds
And birds rejoice with dawn of day

My eyes open from slumber, still
On this side of eternity
I contemplate your loving grace
Your peace my soul seeks earnestly

I offer you my gratitude
With poet's heart I give you thanks
Through songs of love you've given me
I give you back my very best

Follow-Up Exercises

Jot down any thoughts, reactions, feelings, and insights that occurred to you while you engaged in this Spiritual Renewal process for today. You might want to let these questions guide your journaling.

1. In what ways, if any, did the process of critical reflection resonate with you?

2. As you completed the exercises, did you sense any tension in the equilibrium of your mind, body, and spirit?

3. What insights, changes, or new directions have you discerned?

4 In your spare time, use one of the reflective tools (i.e., storytelling, letter writing, theological reflection) to help you make sense of the spiritual insights you gained today.

Closing Prayer

End your devotional time by communicating with God through prayer. Remember that our prayers don't need to be long, creative, or dramatic. They need only to be sincere. Sometimes the simplest prayers say it all.

Chapter Eighteen
Radical Love

Centering

Find a quiet place where you can relax and be alone for a while. Breathe deeply—inhale and exhale in rhythmic fashion. Gather your mental, physical, and spiritual faculties as you listen with expectancy and invite the Holy Spirit to give you a refreshed perspective.

Prayer

Sustaining God, I put my hope in you both now and forevermore. I cast my cares on you and have confidence that you are in control. Amen.

Focus Scripture: Matthew 6:24–34

Focus Questions

Consider the following guiding questions.

1. What do I think the writer wants to convey in this text? What is the central idea?

2. What is my understanding of trying to "serve two masters"?

3. What does this scripture reveal about my relationship with God?

4. In what specific ways can I apply the lessons of this scripture to my daily living?

5. In what ways, if any, do I perceive the Holy Spirit at work in this scripture?

6. In what ways, if any, does this text suggest a link between mind, body, and spirit?

Silent Contemplation Exercises

During Silent Contemplation find a comfortable place where you can be silent, still, and receptive for several minutes without interruption. Quietly reflect on how you believe the Holy Spirit is guiding you to understand the message of today's scripture. Try to respond to each of the focus questions. Then spend a few minutes recording your thoughts in your journal.

Author's Critical Reflection

In the Matthew account, Jesus has just finished preaching the Sermon on the Mount and has warned those listening about being overly pious. He has also cautioned them about storing up treasures on earth where they are subject to deterioration and theft. Jesus tells the listeners that they cannot serve two masters—they cannot serve both God and wealth. Attempting to do so, of course, causes a conflict of interest, and results in hating the one master and loving the other. Jesus also tells the listeners that they should not be overly concerned with the matters of this life. In verse 25 the scripture reads: "Therefore I tell you, do not worry about your life, what you will eat or drink; or about your body, what you will wear. Is not life more important than food, and the body more important than clothes?" From time to time, in the process of preparing us for Christian ministry, God strategically and providentially places in our paths people to serve as mentors. In my case, this person was a woman who taught me about radical love—the kind that is stone solid and never ending. Not only did she speak the words; she daily acted out this simple precept. And in doing so—in her own quiet way—she carried the banner of radical discipleship in the name of love.

Whenever I think about this scripture, I think about my Great Aunt Ruth. Born in Mississippi in 1908, Ruth and her husband were among the many people who migrated to the Chicago area around the 1930s and 1940s. When they first embarked on this great migration, they didn't know what would face them when they arrived. They stepped out on faith and trusted God to provide the rest. There was nothing physically remarkable about Ruth. She was only five feet three inches tall. Her appearance was very plain. She didn't go to church much—as far as she was concerned, the congregation consisted of a bunch of hypocrites who were very much into materialism and extremely judgmental against people who were not like them. Ruth was not materially wealthy but she lacked for nothing. And what she had, she humbly shared with other people. Her lifestyle was simple; her heart was pure. Though she was meek and unassuming, her spirit was huge. She didn't worry too much about how she was going to make it from day to day, for she possessed this abiding faith that God would provide. In my opinion, she was one of God's lilies, clothed in beauty and touched by the grace of God—whom she loved with all her heart.

Back in the early 1950s the community Ruth lived in was a curious blend of rural reminiscence and suburban promise. Even though this community was considered to be a suburb of Chicago in the 1950s, many of the incoming residents kept animals—in Ruth's case that included a hound dog, several chickens, a rooster, and a goat. And in those days, most of the residents in the community still had outhouses.

Ruth loved the land and boldly coexisted with nature. I believe that nurturing this relationship with nature was one of the ways she expressed her love of God. In her part of town, cyclone fences separated the yards from each other. Some of the fences were draped lushly with vines and other creeping plants. From time to time, harmless snakes would intertwine themselves among the leaves. But Ruth was undaunted by such minor annoyances. Her Mississippi soul used to march right up to the fence, grab the snake by the tail, and, with a snap of her wrist, she would whip the snake over into the adjacent field before the slithering creature had a chance to hiss. I was a little girl at the time and all I could say was "Wow!"

In verse 26 of our Matthew account, Jesus tells the listeners to "look at the birds of the air; they do not sow or reap or store away in barns, and yet your heavenly Father feeds them. Are you not much more valuable than they?" Ruth understood this message very well. She had a way with vegetables. If you could eat it, Ruth could grow it—collard greens, tomatoes, peppers, rhubarb, corn, and tall stalks of okra. She taught us how to plant and water and weed. She taught us about good bugs and bad. Every year at harvest time, she shared her bounty with those around her, especially with the ones she loved.

Verse 33 reminds the listeners that if they seek first [the Kingdom of God] and God's righteousness, their material needs will be taken care of as well. Ruth indeed sought first the Kingdom of God by devoting her attention to the lives of other people. Near the end of her own life, Ruth spent her days tending to the needs of my brother, her great nephew, who had lived a troubled life. Having been labeled a loser and treated as a pariah, he found himself lost, alone, and homeless. He literally had no place to go. Ruth took him in, obeying God's command to love our neighbors as ourselves. She gave him a place to sleep, food to eat, and clothes to wear. She shared with him everything she had, cherishing him as if he were her own son. And I believe she saved his life in the process by giving him hope. Ruth was a model of selflessness, trust, and generosity. She was one of God's lilies, clothed in God's grace. And God cared for her all the days of her life. I thank God for lilies. I thank God for Ruth. I thank God for these memories.

Author's CREST

Wake Up, Little Girl
© 2008 by Lorrie C. Reed

Wake up, little girl; go find your peace
It does not reside in your busyness
You will not find it in your knowledge base
Nor does it live at the bottom of that bottle

Wake up, little girl; your peace awaits you
Go unpack your bags for the journey
In search of treasure hidden in your soul of souls
In the place where the Spirit lives

Follow-Up Exercises

Jot down any thoughts, reactions, feelings, and insights that occurred to you while you engaged in this Spiritual Renewal process for today. You might want to let these questions guide your journaling.

1. In what ways, if any, did the process of critical reflection resonate with you?

2. As you completed the exercises, did you sense any tension in the equilibrium of your mind, body, and spirit?

3. What insights, changes, or new directions have you discerned?

4. In your spare time, use one of the reflective tools (i.e., storytelling, letter writing, theological reflection) to help you make sense of the spiritual insights you gained today.

Closing Prayer

End your devotional time by communicating with God through prayer. Remember that our prayers don't need to be long, creative, or dramatic. They need only to be sincere. Sometimes the simplest prayers say it all.

Chapter Nineteen

Sanctuary

Centering

Find a quiet place where you can relax and be alone for a while. Breathe deeply—inhale and exhale in rhythmic fashion. Gather your mental, physical, and spiritual faculties as you listen with expectancy and invite the Holy Spirit to give you a refreshed perspective.

Prayer

O Lord my God, I ask nothing for myself today. I simply want to thank you for another opportunity to give you honor and sing your praise. I adore you, Lord, and I thank you for considering even me and for protecting me by your grace. Amen.

Focus Scripture: Psalm 8

Focus Questions

Consider the following guiding questions.

1. What do I think the writer wants to convey in this text? What is the central idea?

2. What does this scripture reveal about the writer?

3. What does this scripture reveal about God?

4. In what specific ways can I apply the lessons of this scripture to my daily living?

5. In what ways, if any, do I perceive the Holy Spirit at work in this scripture?

6. In what ways, if any, does this text suggest a link between mind, body, and spirit?

Silent Contemplation Exercises

During Silent Contemplation find a comfortable place where you can be silent, still, and receptive for several minutes without interruption. Quietly reflect on how you believe the Holy Spirit is guiding you to understand the message of today's scripture. Try to respond to each of the focus questions. Then spend a few minutes recording your thoughts in your journal.

Author's Critical Reflection

Today's scripture speaks of the wonder of God's creation. It starts out by saying: "O Lord, our Lord, how majestic is your name in all the earth!" There was a time in my life before I retired from the field of education that I used to commute long distances on an interstate highway to get to work. I would leave early in the morning, off to my destination. Much of the time I drove along in silence, marveling at the beauty and intricacy of what God had spoken into existence at the beginning of time. It was during these commutes that I came to understand that God's creation truly is majestic.

The second part of today's scripture focuses on that sense of insignificance that I felt as I drove along. For example, verses 3 and 4 say: "When I consider your heavens, the work of your fingers, the moon and the stars, which you have set in place, what is man that you are mindful of him, the son of man that you care for him?" What is humankind, indeed, in the face of God's magnificence? Yes, God has made us a little lower than the angels. God has crowned us with glory and honor. God has given us dominion over all that God has made. But in the broader scheme of things, what is humankind that God is even mindful of us? How do our meager accomplishments measure up against what God has done? The answer is that they don't.

One of the trips I made on a regular basis took me from east to west as I drove from Chicago to DeKalb on Interstate 88, which is now the Ronald Reagan Expressway. I had to leave my house before dawn to get to a meeting or a class on time. It's interesting to note that on my way, the landscape changed many times. The trip was about 90 miles, and I used to divide it up into legs to make it more manageable. On the first leg of the trip, the landscape changed from vacant lots and concrete slabs to suburban residential communities. On the second leg of the trip, the concrete and congestion began to yield to shopping malls and office plazas. But it was on the third leg of the trip that something special always happened. Instead of office buildings, farmland stretched as far as the eye could see. And there was space all around to breathe and think and feel and to savor the beauty of what God had made.

I particularly remember the aromas of early spring. There were many open fields emitting the smells of freshly mowed grass or freshly cut crops. There were the scents of lilacs and clover and that unmistakable scent of the ground thawing in the early spring or the smell of rain in the air and the promise of new life that it all brought to mind. The colors also were vibrant. Purples and yellows and reds and greens and rich browns set against the backdrop of the blue, blue sky, sometimes dotted with clouds, sometimes not.

And there were horses. Every time I passed milepost 103, I looked to my left and saw four or five horses just standing in the field. They always faced south for some reason. This sounds silly, but every time I passed them I would wave and say "Hi, horses." They never answered back, of course. But their very presence represented stability and wonder.

I remember one trip in particular. The highway stretched out in a flat plain ahead of me as I drove on this narrow stretch of road. And above it all was the endless sky spanning forever in all directions, unmarred by smokestacks or high-rise buildings. On that day as I looked through the windshield, I saw the sky, so clear and pure and endless, as it hung in the eternal space all around me. I was so struck by the beauty and the majesty of it all that I gasped out loud and thanked God for the Divine portrait that I beheld. But there was still more. I glanced in my rearview mirror. And there was the sun peeking over the horizon at the dawn to pay honor to the new day. The word *awesome* does not do justice to the beauty of that moment. I felt so blessed, but at the same time I felt absolutely insignificant in the broader scheme of things. And all I could say was Lord, Our Lord, how excellent is your name in all the earth! What a blessing!

During those long trips, I reached several conclusions. God is greater than our insecurities. God is greater than our pain. God is greater than our sorrow. God is greater than our disappointments. God is the author of time, the creator of our beginnings, and keeper of our endings. God is greater than the great! God is stronger than the strong! God is our all in all! And those things became very clear to me on the days that I drove from east to west in those mornings just before dawn. How honored I felt. How humbled I felt in God's magnificent presence. And I had a strong sense of receiving a blessing that was tailor made just for me. The only thing I can say in response is "Lord, O Lord, how majestic is your name in all the earth!" Amen.

Author's CREST

Joy
© 2008 by Lorrie C. Reed

I had no frame of reference
For recognizing joy
Then you erased my sadness
As I embraced your love

You breathed into my spirit
Your wind of hope and peace
Transforming me from inside
My joy is now complete

Follow-Up Exercises

Jot down any thoughts, reactions, feelings, and insights that occurred to you while you engaged in this Spiritual Renewal process for today. You might want to let these questions guide your journaling.

1. In what ways, if any, did the process of critical reflection resonate with you?

2. As you completed the exercises, did you sense any tension in the equilibrium of your mind, body, and spirit?

3. What insights, changes, or new directions have you discerned?

4. In your spare time, use one of the reflective tools (i.e., storytelling, letter writing, theological reflection) to help you make sense of the spiritual insights you gained today.

Closing Prayer

End your devotional time by communicating with God through prayer. Remember that our prayers don't need to be long, creative, or dramatic. They need only to be sincere. Sometimes the simplest prayers say it all.

A Special Invitation—
You Are Invited!

Through God's amazing grace we are offered forgiveness of sin, eternal salvation, and new life in Jesus Christ. God loved the world so much that he sent Jesus, his only Son, to save humankind from sin and death (John 3:16). And through Christ, by the power of the Holy Spirit, God will establish an eternal Kingdom characterized by justice, love, and peace for the whole world (1 Corinthians 15:24–28; Matthew 25:31–46).

But that's not all. Romans 10:13 tells us that *everyone* who calls on the name of the Lord shall be saved. The scripture further states: "For it is with your heart that you believe and are justified, and it is with your mouth that you confess and are saved" (Romans 10:10, NIV). This process of salvation begins on earth and ends in heaven. All we are asked to do is repent and believe (Romans 10:9–13). When we believe we willingly invite Jesus into our lives.

If you do not know Jesus as your personal Savior, I invite you to get acquainted with him. Salvation is only a prayer away.

> "Loving God, I confess that I am a sinner, and I am sorry for my sin. I believe that Jesus can save me. I believe that through his death and resurrection I am forgiven, and that my faith in Jesus is sufficient for my salvation. Thank you Lord, for saving me and forgiving me! Amen!"

The Apostles' Creed

The Apostles' Creed has stood for centuries as a general statement of doctrine in many Christian denominations. It is reproduced here for your edification.

I believe in God, the Father Almighty,
  the Creator of heaven and earth,
  and in Jesus Christ, His only Son, our Lord:
Who was conceived of the Holy Spirit,
    born of the Virgin Mary,
    suffered under Pontius Pilate,
    was crucified, died, and was buried.
He descended into hell.
The third day He arose again from the dead.
He ascended into heaven
    and sits at the right hand of God the Father
  Almighty,
    whence He shall come to judge the living and the
  dead.
I believe in the Holy Spirit, the holy catholic church*,
    the communion of saints,
    the forgiveness of sins,
    the resurrection of the body,
    and life everlasting. Amen.

*The word "catholic" refers to the universal church of the Lord Jesus Christ.

Closing Prayer

Precious and Loving God, who speaks to me in many ways, teach me how to relax and to let go of all the things that burden me down. Put me in a frame of mind to receive the blessings of peace and joy I am certain you have in store for me as I reflect on your Word. In your Holy Name I pray, Amen.

Benediction

Dear friends, may God bless you richly as you embark on this journey of daily devotion for your spiritual renewal! May the peace of Jesus Christ be with you always!

Bibliography

Abbott, J., R. Johnson, and J. Kaziol-McLain. "Domestic Violence against Women: Incidence and Prevalence in an Emergency Department Population." *Journal of the American Medical Association*, (1995): 272, 1763–1767.

American Red Cross. *Helping Young Children Cope with Trauma*. Retrieved July 20, 2007 from http://www.redcross.org/

Anderson, Vera. *A Woman like You: The Face of Domestic Violence*. Retrieved March 30, 2009 from http://www.veraanderson.com/thebook.htm

Bancroft, Lundy. 2002. *Why Does He Do That? Inside the Minds of Angry and Controlling Men*. New York: Berkley Books.

Berliner, L., and J. R. Conte. The effects of disclosure and intervention on sexually abused children. *Child Abuse & Neglect*, (1995), 19: 371–84.

Berry, Dawn Bradley. *The Domestic Violence Sourcebook*. 3rd ed. Lincolnwood: Lowell House, 2000.

Bureau of Justice Statistics. *Intimate Violence*. U. S. Department of Justice. Office of Justice Programs. 2005 report. Retrieved December 12, 2007 from http://ojp.usdoj.gov/bjs/cvict_c.htm#intimate

Burley-Allen, Madelyn. *Listening the Forgotten Skill*. Hoboken, NJ: John Wiley and Sons, 1982.

Bush, Joseph E., Jr. *Gentle Shepherding: Pastoral Ethics and Leadership*. St. Louis: Chalice Press, 2006.

Butler, Lee H., Jr. *Liberating Our Dignity, Saving Our Lives*. St. Louis: Chalice Press, 2006.

Chicago Metropolitan Battered Women's Network (CMBWN). *Responding to Domestic Violence: An Interfaith Guide to Prevention and Intervention*, Chicago, IL: Author, 2005, 11–13.

Chicago Metropolitan Battered Women's Network. *Domestic Violence 40-Hour Training.* Chicago: Author, 2005.

Conte, J. R., Wolf, S., and T. Smith. What sexual offenders tell us about prevention strategies. Child Abuse & Neglect, (1989), 13: 293–301.

Duncan, Stephen F. 50 Stress Busting Ideas for Your Well-being. Montana State University Extension Service. Available online. Retrieved August 11, 2008 from http://www.montana.edu/wwwpb/pubs/mt200016.html

Erickson, J., and A. Henderson. "Diverging realities: Abused women and their children. In J. Campbell (Ed.), *Empowering survivors of abuse: Health Care for Battered Women and Their Children* (pp. 138–155). Thousand Oaks, CA: Sage, 1998.

Everson, M. D., and B. W. Boat. False allegations of sexual abuse by children and adolescents. *Journal of the American Academy of Child and Adolescent Psychiatry.* (1989), 28: 230-5.

Ferrato, Donna. *Living with the Enemy.* Retrieved March 30, 2009 from http://www.donnaferrato.com/biography.php

Finkelhor, D., and J. Dziuba-Leatherman. Children as Victims of Violence: A National Survey. *Pediatrics,* (1994), 94(4):413–420.

Fortune, Marie M. "The Transformation of Suffering: A Biblical and Theological Perspective." In. Carol J. Adams, and Mary M. Fortune, Eds., *Violence against Women and Children: A Christian Theological Source Book* (pp. 85–91). New York: Continuum Publishing, 1995.

Fortune, Marie M. *Sexual Violence: The Sin Revisited.* Cleveland: Pilgrim Press, 2005.

Grant, Jacqueline. "Freeing the Captives: The Imperative of Womanist Theology." In Iva Carruthers, Frederick Haynes, and Jeremiah Wright, Jr., Eds., *Blow the Trumpet in Zion* (pp. 86–90). Minneapolis: Fortress Press, 2005.

Greenwald, Barry. *Abnormal Psychology Home Page,* University of Illinois—Chicago. Retrieved March 21, 2009 from http://www.uic.edu/classes/psych/psych270/PTSD.htm

Hanson, R. F., H. S. Resnick, B. E. Saunders, D. G. Kilpatrick, and C. Best. Factors related to the reporting of childhood rape. *Child Abuse & Neglect*, (1999),23: 559–69.

Healey, Joseph and Donald Sybertz. *Towards an African Narrative Theology.* Maryknoll, NY: Orbis Books, 1996, 192.

Herman, Judith. *Trauma and Recovery.* New York: Basic Books, 1992.

Hunter, J. A., D. W. Goodwin, and R. J. Wilson. Attributions of blame in child sexual abuse victims: An analysis of age and gender influences. *Journal of Child Sexual Abuse*, (1992), 1: 75–89.

Illinois Coalition against Domestic Violence. *Handbook for Domestic Violence Victims.* Springfield, IL: Author, 2001.

Institute on Domestic Violence in the African American Community (IDVAAC). "Fact Sheet on Intimate Partner Violence (IPV) in the African American Community". *Institute on Domestic Violence in the African American Community (IDVAAC). University of Minnesota.* Retrieved December 12, 2007 from http://www.dvinstitute.org/media/factdv.htm

Jenks, E. B. *Searching for Autoethnograpic Credibility: Reflections from a Mom with a Notepad.* In A. P. Bochner & C. Ellis (Eds.), *Ethnographically Speaking: Autoethography, Literature, and Aesthetics* (pp. 170–186). New York: AltaMira Press, 2002.

Jinkins, Michael. *Letters to New Pastors.* Grand Rapids, MI: Eerdmans Publishing Company, 2006.

Johnson, Abigail. *Reflecting with God.* Herndon, VA: The Alban Institute, 2004.

Jones, Kirk Byron. *Rest in the Storm: Self-Care Strategies for Clergy and Other Caregivers.* Valley Forge, PA: Judson Press, 2001.

Just, Felix, *Household Codes in the New Testament*, 2005. Retrieved June 18, 2008, from http://catholic-resources.org/Bible/Epistles-HouseholdCodes.htm

Kilpatrick, D. G., C. N. Edmunds, and A. Seymour. *Rape in America: A report to the National Victim Center.* Arlington VA: National Victim Center, 1992.

Laura Russell, "Posttraumatic Stress Disorder DSM-IV™ Diagnosis & Criteria -- 309.81Posttraumatic Stress Disorder. Retrieved July 3, 2008 from http://www.mental-health-today.com/ptsd/dsm. htm).

Lawson, L., and M. Chaffin. False negatives in sexual abuse disclosure interviews. *Journal of Interpersonal Violence*, (1992), 7: 532–42.

Leadership Council on Child Abuse and Interpersonal Violence (LCCAIV). Eight Common Myths about Child Sexual Abuse. Retrieved March 30, 2009 from http://www.leadershipcouncil. org/1/res/csa_myths.html

LeBaron, Michelle. Communication Tools for Understanding Cultural Differences. *Beyond Intractability*, eds. Guy Burgess and Heidi Burgess. Conflict Research Consortium, University of Colorado, Boulder. Posted: June 2003 http://www. beyondintractability.org/essay/communication_tools/.

Levine, Peter A. *Walking the Tiger: Healing Trauma.* Berkeley CA: North Atlantic Books, 1997.

Lyon, T. D. Scientific Support for Expert Testimony on Child Sexual Abuse Accommodation. *In* J.R. Conte (Ed.), *Critical issues in child sexual abuse* (pp. 107–138). Newbury Park, CA: Sage. (online: http://www.law.duke.edu/shell/cite.pl?65+Law+&+Con temp.+Probs.+97+(Winter+2002)

Lyon, T. D. The new wave of suggestibility research: A critique. *Cornell Law Review*, (1999), 84: 1004–1087.

Lyon, T.D. Let's not exaggerate the suggestibility of children. *Court Review*, (2001), 28 (3): 12–14. (online: http://aja.ncsc.dni.us/ courtrv/cr38-3/CR38-3Lyon.pdf)

Nason-Clark, Nancy. *The Battered Wife: How Christians Confront Family Violence.* Louisville: Westminster John Knox Press, 1994.

National Domestic Violence Hotline. *Official Website.* Retrieved December 12, 2007 from http://www.ndvh.org/educate/ what_is_dv.html

Paul, Miki. (2004). Clinical Implications in Healing from Domestic Violence: A Case Study. *American Psychologist*, 59(8), November 2004: 809–816.

Pipe, M. E., and G. S. Goodman. Elements of secrecy: Implications for children's testimony. *Behavioral Sciences & the Law*, (1991), 9: 33–41.

Polin, Vicki, Michael J. Salamon, and Ha'ama Yehuda. *Spirituality, Sexuality, and How Survivors of Childhood Sexual Abuse Experience God*. Retrieved March 30, 2009 from http://www. theawarenesscenter.org/SpiritualitySexuality.pdf

Presbyterian Church (PCUSAa). *Turn Mourning into Dancing! A Policy Statement on Healing Domestic Violence and Study Guide*. Advisory Committee on Social Witness Policy of the General Assembly Council. Louisville: Office of the General Assembly, 2001.

Presbyterian Church (PCUSAb). Office of Spiritual Formation. 2003. Retrieved July 20, 2007, from http://www.pcusa.org/ spiritualformation/index.htm

Robinson, Lori S. *I Will Survive: The African-American Guide to Healing from Sexual Assault and Abuse*. Emeryville, CA: Seal P, 2003.

Robinson, Marilynne. "Psalm Eight." In *The Death of Adam: Essays in Modern Thought*. Boston, Houghton Mifflin, 1998, 227–244.

Salter, A. C. *Predators: Pedophiles, Rapists and Other Sex Offenders: Who They Are, How They Operate, and How We Can Protect Ourselves and Our Children*. New York: Basic Books, 2003.

Saunders, D. Child Custody Decisions in Families Experiencing Woman Abuse, *Social Work*, (39)1, 1994, 51–59.

Sauzier, M. Disclosure of child sexual abuse: For better or for worse. *Psychiatric Clinics of North America*, (1989), 12: 455–69.

Seligman, M. E. P. Why is there so much depression today? In R. E. Ingram (Ed.), Contemporary psychoanalytical approaches to depression (pp. 1-9). New York: Plenum, 1990.

Sheldrake, Philip. *A Brief History of Spirituality*. Malden, MA: Blackwell Publishing, 2007.

Sjoberg, R. L., and F. Lindblad. Limited disclosure of sexual abuse in children whose experiences were documented by videotape. *American Journal of Psychiatry*, (2002), 159: 312–4

Smith, Brenda V. "Battering, Forgiveness, and Redemption". In *Domestic Violence at the Margins*, ed. Natalie J. Sokoloff. New Brunswick: Rutgers UP, 321–329, 2006.

Smith, D. W., Letourneau, E. J., Saunders, B. E., Kilpatrick, D. G., Resnick, H. S., and C. L. Best. Delay in disclosure of childhood rape: Results from a national survey. *Child Abuse & Neglect*, (2000), 24: 273–87.

Stanford University. *Sexual Assault and Relationship Abuse Prevention and Support at Stanford.* Facts and Myths Concerning Sexual Assault. Retrieved March 21, 2009 from http://www.stanford.edu/group/svab/myths.shtml

Thistlethwaite, Susan Brooks. "Battered Women and the Bible: From Subjection to Liberation." *Christianity and Crisis* 41.8 (1981): 308–313.

U. S. Conference of Mayors. *A Status Report on Hunger and Homelessness in America's Cities: A 25-City Survey.* VIA National Network to End Domestic Violence, December, 2003.

Walker, Lenore E. A. *Abused Women and Survivor Therapy.* Washington, D.C.: American Psychological Association, 1994.

Walker, Lenore E. A. *The Battered Woman Syndrome.* 2nd ed. New York: Springer, 2000.

Watkins, B. and A. Bentovim. The sexual abuse of male children and adolescents: A review of current research. *Journal of Child Psychology and Psychiatry*, (1992), 33: 197–248.

Webster, Merriam. *Ninth New Collegiate Dictionary.* Springfield, MA: Author, 1984.

West, Carolyn M., ed. *Violence in the Lives of Black Women: Battered Black and Blue.* New York: Haworth, 2002.

White, Jenelle, L. "Anti-oppression Theory." *CALCASA Support for Survivors,* 211–215.

Whitfield, Charles L. *Healing the Child Within: Discovery and Recovery for Adult Children of Dysfunctional Families.* Deerfield Beach, FL: Health Communications, Inc., 2006.

Williams, Rowan. *Where God Happens: Discovering Christ in One Another.* Boston: New Seeds, 2005.

Wilmore, Gayraud S.. *Black Religion and Black Radicalism: An Interpretation of the Religious History of Afro-American People.* Maryknoll, NY: Orbis Books, 1990.

Wimberly, Edward P. *Claiming God, Reclaiming Dignity.* Nashville: Abingdon, 2003.

World News. (www.abcnews.com, World News with Charles Gibson, June 12, 2008).

Wright, N. T. 2002. Romans 5:1–5: "Peace, Patience, and Hope: Commentary." In *New Interpreter's Bible: A Commentary in Twelve Volumes, Volume X,* ed. Leander Keck, 515–517. Nashville: Abingdon Press.

Zastrow, Charles. *Introduction to Social Work and Social Welfare: Empowering People,* 9th Edition. Belmont, CA: Thomson Higher Education, 2008, 506.

Endnotes

1. Palmer, Parker J. *Let Your Life Speak: Listening for the Voice of Vocation.* San Francisco: Jossey-Bass. 2000, 12.

2. Palmer, Parker J. *Let Your Life Speak: Listening for the Voice of Vocation.* San Francisco: Jossey-Bass. 2000, 26–27.

3. Palmer, Parker J. *Let Your Life Speak: Listening for the Voice of Vocation.* San Francisco: Jossey-Bass. 2000, 10.

4. Thurman, Howard. *Disciplines of the Spirit* (10th edition). Richmond, IN: Friends United Press, 2003, p. 25–26.

5. McKim, Donald K. *Westminster Dictionary of Theological Terms.* Louisville: Westminster John Knox Press, 1996, 267.

6. PCUSA (Presbyterian Church (USA)). Office of Spiritual Formation. 2003. Retrieved 20. July, 2007, from http://www.pcusa.org/spiritualformation/index.htm

7. Marilyn Robinson's insightful essay describes her process of spiritual development. Information in this section pertains to her essay. The entire essay may be found at: Robinson, Marilynne. "Psalm Eight." In The Death of Adam: Essays in Modern Thought. Boston, Houghton Mifflin, 1998, 227–244.

8. Robinson, Marilynne. *Ibid.,* 228.

9. Robinson, Marilynne. *Ibid.,* 240.

10. PCUSA. 2003. Presbyterian Church (USA). Office of Spiritual Formation. Retrieved 20. July, 2007, from http://www.pcusa.org/spiritualformation/index.htm

11. As quoted in PCUSA. 2003. Presbyterian Church (USA). Office of Spiritual Formation. Retrieved July 20, 2007, from http://www.pcusa.org/spiritualformation/index.htm

12. Rowan Williams is the current Archbishop of Canterbury and has described Monasticism in his book: *Where God Happens.* Williams, Rowan. *Where God Happens: Discovering Christ in One Another.* Boston: New Seeds, 2005, 27.

13. Williams, Rowan, 2005, 128.

14. New Advent Catholic Encyclopedia. 2003. Retrieved October 31. 2006. from the *Official Website* at http://www.newadvent.org.

15. Meinardus, Otto, F. A. *Monks and Monestaries of the Egyptian Desert*, Rev. ed. (Cairo, Egypt: American University in Cairo UP, 1989), ix.

16. Meinardus, Otto F. A. 1989, 1.

17. Hanrahan, James. "St. Basil the Great Part 1: The Congregation of St. Basil." In *The Life of Saint Basil*. The Basilian Press Toronto, 1979. 31. Oct. 2006. http://www.basilian.org/Publica/StBasil/Stbasil1.htm

18. Williams, Rowan. *Where God Happens: Discovering Christ in One Another.* Boston: New Seeds, 2005, 124.

19. Edwards, Tilden. *Spiritual Director, Spiritual Companion: Guide to Tending the Soul.* New York: Paulist Press, 2001.

20. Edwards, Tilden, 2001, 45

21. The information in this section is taken from Society of Jesus in their extensive reporting on "The Spiritual Exercises of St. Ignatius". Society of Jesus. 2006. "The Spiritual Exercises of St. Ignatius" *Official Website of the Society of Jesus.* Retrieved 4. August, 2007, from http://www.nwjesuits.org/JesuitSpirituality/SpiritualExercises.html

22. Extensive information about St. Teresa of Avila is available from Catholic First. The descriptions in this section are taken from their official website. Catholic First. 2006. "Interior Castle", St. Teresa of Avila. *Catholic Information Center on the Web.* Retrieved 4. August 2007. from http://www.catholicfirst.com/thefaith/catholicclassics/stteresa/castle/interiorcastle.cfm

23. Catholic First. 2006.

24. Gayraud S. Wilmore. *Black Religion and Black Radicalism: An Interpretation of the Religious History of Afro-American People.* Maryknoll, NY: Orbis Books, 1990, 15.

25. Gayraud S. Wilmore. *Black Religion and Black Radicalism: An Interpretation of the Religious History of Afro-American People.* Maryknoll, NY: Orbis Books, 1990, 15.

26. Joseph Healey and Donald Sybertz. *Towards an African Narrative Theology.* Maryknoll, NY: Orbis Books, 1996, 192.

27. Philip Sheldrake. *A Brief History of Spirituality.* Malden, MA: Blackwell Publishing, 2007.

28. Gayraud S. Wilmore. *Black Religion and Black Radicalism: An Interpretation of the Religious History of Afro-American People.* Maryknoll, NY: Orbis Books, 1990, 7.

29. Gayraud S. Wilmore. *Black Religion and Black Radicalism: An Interpretation of the Religious History of Afro-American People.* Maryknoll, NY: Orbis Books, 1990, 9.

30. Thurman, Howard. *Disciplines of the Spirit* (10th edition). Richmond, IN: Friends United Press, 2003, 29.

31. Thurman, Howard. *Ibid.,* 29.

32. Thurman, Howard. *Ibid.,* 63.

33. See Luke 6:44, NKJV.

34. See Galatians 5:22-23, NKJV.

35. See, for example, John 1:1–4.

36. See, for example, Psalm 40:3.

37. See Col 1:9–12, NIV.

38. Answers.com (Retrieved 7/26/2008. from Answers.com at http://www.answers.com/topic/mental-health)

39. Answers.com. *Ibid.*

40. Westgate, Charlene E. (September, 1996). Spiritual wellness and depression. *Journal of Counseling and Development, 75*(1), 26–35.

41. ELCA. 1997. *Ministerial Health and Wellness: The Wholeness Wheel.* Retrieved 7/26/2008. from http://www.elca.org/Growing-In-Faith/Vocation/Rostered-Leadership/Leadership-Support/Health/Wholeness-Wheel.aspx

42. ELCA. 1997.

43. Bryant, Stephen D. Bryant, Ed. *The Upper Room Daily Devotional Guide.* Nashville, TN: The Upper Room, July–August 2008, 29.

44. Eck, Diana. *Encountering God.* Boston: Beacon Press, 2003, 133.

45. Eck, Diana. *Ibid.,* 119.

46. Eck, Diana. *Ibid.,* 133.

47. Eck, Diana. *Encountering God.* Boston: Beacon Press, 2003, 151.

48. Marshall, Jay. "Integrity Described". *Alive Now* Volume 38. (September/October) No. 5, 2008, p. 52.

49. See 1. John 3:24.

50. Boff, Leonardo. *Ecology & Liberation: A New Paradigm.* Maryknoll: Orbis, 1995, 7

51. Boff, Leonardo. *Ibid.,* 7.

52. Thurman, Howard. *Disciplines of the Spirit* (10th edition). Richmond, IN: Friends United Press, 2003, 22.

53. Thurman, Howard. *Disciplines of the Spirit* (10th edition). Richmond, IN: Friends United Press, 2003, 96.

54. Monk Moses, "The Community of the Desert and the Loneliness of the Cities," *Greek Orthodox Archdiocese* Website. Retrieved 12. Dec. 2006. from http://www.goarch.org/en/ourfaith/introduction/

55. Monk Moses, "The Community of the Desert and the Loneliness of the Cities," *Greek Orthodox Archdiocese* Website. Retrieved 12. Dec. 2006. from http://www.goarch.org/en/ourfaith/introduction/, 61.

56. Thurman, Howard. *Ibid.,* 88.

57. Thurman, Howard. *Ibid.,* 95–96.

58. Contemplative Outreach, "Centering Prayer Overview". Official website. Retrieved July 11, 2008. from http://www.centeringprayer.com/docs/MethodCP2008.pdf

59. Contemplative Outreach, "Centering Prayer Overview". Official website. Retrieved July 11, 2008. from http://www.centeringprayer.com/docs/MethodCP2008.pdf

60. Rowan Williams. *Where God Happens: Discovering Christ in One Another.* (Boston: New Seeds, 2005), 82.

61. Kiesinger, C. E. My father's shoes: The therapeutic value of narrative reframing. In A. Bochner & C. Ellis (Eds.), *Ethnographically Speaking: Autoethnography, Literature, and Aesthetics* (pp. 95–114). Walnut Creek, CA: AltaMira Press, 2002.

62. Butler, Lee H., Jr. *Liberating Our Dignity, Saving Our Lives.* St. Louis: Chalice Press, 2006, as cited in Wimberly, Edward P. *Claiming God, Reclaiming Dignity.* Nashville: Abingdon, 2003, 11.

63. Wimberly, Edward P. *Claiming God, Reclaiming Dignity.* Nashville: Abingdon, 2003, 40

64. Wimberly, Edward P. *Ibid.,* 119–120.

65. Butler, Lee H., Jr. *Liberating Our Dignity, Saving Our Lives.* St. Louis: Chalice Press, 2006, 161

66. Johnson, Abigail. *Reflecting with God.* Herndon, VA: The Alban Institute, 2004

67. Jacques, Genevieve. *Beyond impunity: An ecumenical approach to truth, justice, and reconciliation.* Geneva: WCC, 2000, 16.

68. Whitfield, Charles L. *Healing the Child Within: Discovery and Recovery for Adult Children of Dysfunctional Families.* Deerfield Beach, FL: Health Communications, Inc., 2006, p. 97.

69. Jinkins, Michael. *Letters to New Pastors.* Grand Rapids, MI: Eerdmans Publishing Company, 2006, xi.

70. Kiesinger, 2002.

71. Jennifer Hollowell. *Keeping a Journal: The Importance of Daily Writing.* March 27, 2007. Suite 101.com. Retrieved March 22, 2009. from http://self-awareness.suite101.com/article.cfm/keeping_a_journal#ixzz0AaD8OmUx

72. See John 14:26, NIV.

73. See James 3:17. and John 14:27.

74. Some of those Internet sources are listed in the appendix of this book.

75. See 1. Corinthians 10:13.

76. See, for example, Ecclesiastes 4:9–12.

77. Merriam Webster, *Ninth New Collegiate Dictionary.* Springfield, MA: Author, 1984.

78. Whitfield, Charles L. *Healing the Child Within: Discovery and Recovery for Adult Children of Dysfunctional Families.* Deerfield Beach, FL: Health Communications, Inc., 2006, 85.

79. Levine, Peter A. *Walking the Tiger: Healing Trauma.* Berkeley CA: North Atlantic Books, 1997, p. 35.

80. American Red Cross, 2007.

81. Herman, Judith Lewis. *Trauma and recovery: The aftermath of violence from domestic abuse to political terror* ((Previous ed.: 1992) ed.). Basic Books, 1997, 37.

82. Herman, Judith Lewis, 37.

83. Bancroft 2002.

84. Fortune 2005, 4.

85. Lori Robinson 2003, 370.

86. Lori Robinson 2003, xxiv.

87. L. Robinson 2003, 128.

88. Stephen F. Duncan. 50. Stress Busting Ideas for Your Well-being. Montana State University Extension Service. Available online. Retrieved August 11, 2008. from http://www.montana.edu/wwwpb/pubs/mt200016.html

89. Presbyterian Church (PCUSA), Advisory Committee on Social Witness Policy of the General Assembly Council. *Turn Mourning into Dancing! A Policy Statement on Healing Domestic Violence and Study Guide.* Louisville: Office of the General Assembly, 2001.

90. Chicago Metropolitan Battered Women's Network. *Domestic Violence 40-Hour Training.* Chicago: Author, 2005, 2.3–2.7.

91. Miki Paul, 809–816.

92. Walker, 2000.

93. Berry, 2000, 35–36.

94. Marie M. Fortune. "The Transformation of Suffering: A Biblical and Theological Perspective." *Violence against Women and Children: A Christian Theological Source Book.* Ed. Carol J. Adams and Mary M. Fortune. New York: Continuum Publishing, 1995, 88.

95. Fortune, 1995, 91

96. Fortune, 1995, 88

97. Fortune, 1995, 90.

98. PCUSA.

99. Chicago Metropolitan Battered Women's Network. *Domestic Violence 40-Hour Training.* Chicago: Author, 2005, 2.3–2.7.

100. Laura Russell, "Posttraumatic Stress Disorder DSM-IV™ Diagnosis & Criteria—309.81Posttraumatic Stress Disorder. Retrieved July 3, 2008. from http://www.mental-health-today.com/ptsd/dsm.htm).

101. Malchiodi, 1997.

102. "They promise them freedom, while they themselves are slaves of depravity—for a man is a slave to whatever has mastered him" (2. Peter 2:19).

103. Stephen F. Duncan. 50. Stress Busting Ideas for Your Well-being. Montana State University Extension Service. Available online. Retrieved August 11, 2008. from http://www.montana.edu/wwwpb/pubs/mt200016.html

104. Bernard, J. H. *A Critical and Exegetical Commentary on the Gospel according to St. John* (ICC; Edinburgh: Clark, 1928), 2:348.

About the Author

Lorrie C. Reed recently retired from a 30-year career in the field of education. Her educational leadership included positions as state educational specialist, associate high school principal, director of curriculum and personnel, junior high school principal, and high school English teacher. Later, she taught university courses at the masters and doctoral levels and served as director for an urban education research center. Upon discerning a call to ministry, Dr. Reed opted for early retirement from the university and entered seminary.

Lorrie is a childhood witness of domestic abuse and family violence. Her current vocational mission revolves around a ministry of promoting healing, wholeness, and hope to God's people who have been battered by the storms of life. She has received new life in Jesus Christ and is dedicated to spreading the gospel. She holds a Bachelor of Science degree in English and Secondary Education, a Master of Arts degree in Educational Administration, a Master of Theological Studies, and a PhD in Research Methodology.

LaVergne, TN USA
30 January 2011
214532LV00002B/2/P